RODY KENNY
COURTICE

THE PATTERN OF HER TIMES

RODY KENNY COURTICE

THE PATTERN OF HER TIMES

Curated by
Linda Jansma

THE ROBERT MCLAUGHLIN GALLERY,

OSHAWA

CONTENTS

FOREWORD AND
ACKNOWLEDGMENTS

The time of Rody Kenny Courtice was circumscribed by artistic developments in Canada that meant, among other things, a certain style and identity for "Canadian art." The most familiar example is, of course, the coming to be of The Group of Seven and the Group's manner of landscape painting that even today appears to be the first and most common response to the question: what is Canadian art? The Group's ascendancy and eventual popularity was a significant element of Canada's story, developing out of and yet beyond the old colonial and American influences. But it is only part of that story, and the story is not finished. Many artists, particularly the women it seems, were left somewhat behind and insufficiently considered in modernism's rush forward. Isabel McLaughlin and Alexandra Luke were two such artists, as was Rody Kenny Courtice, one of McLaughlin's closest friends. This exhibition and publication bring a fresh look at Courtice's work, as well as new historical information and important insights into her unique place in Canadian art.

This exhibition is fundamental in a special way for The Robert McLaughlin Gallery, and as we approach our 40th anniversary we are quite mindful of it. Alexandra Luke was one of the founders of the Gallery, especially through her inspired vision and by truly setting the base for our collection with works from her collection. Isabel McLaughlin was the Gallery's most significant principal friend over the years, sustaining it with her unflagging support of exhibitions, public programming and collection. It is right and fitting in several essential ways that we are now taking a long-overdue excursion into the work of Rody Kenny Courtice. Because of Kay Woods, the Gallery's first Curator, our mission was focussed on Canadian modernism; and during the tenure of Joan Murray, Director Emerita of the Gallery, the focus was sustained and broadened with additional attention to the women artists of Canada. They are joined by Curator Linda Jansma whose rare dedication over the last several years to a fuller account of Courtice has brought us this major reappraisal and a new understanding.

The Gallery is grateful for the support of the Government of Canada, through the Department of Canadian Heritage, Museums Assistance Program; the Canada Council for the Arts; the Ontario Arts Council; and the City of Oshawa.

David Aurandt
Executive Director

ACKNOWLEDGMENTS

This exhibition began as an e-mail suggestion by Christopher Varley, who felt there was enough work by Rody Kenny Courtice to do a retrospective. He was right, and I thank him for setting this exhibition in motion. Without the input and support of Rody's son, Paul Courtice, the research process would have been neither as pleasant nor as productive. Paul's willingness to share memories of his mother, as well as works in his collection and photographs was invaluable. A mere "thank you" seems insufficient in acknowledging his role in this exhibition.

Other family members were also extremely helpful: Joan Penney, Karen McCardle and Diane Willemse. Your memories of "Aunt Rody" helped me create, in my own mind, a more complete picture of Rody's character.

Alicia Boutilier's work on the exhibition *4 Women Who Painted in the 1930s and 1940s* for the Carleton University Art Gallery was a primary source for this project. Alicia's willingness to share her vast knowledge of this area of Canadian art was significant. Thank you.

Others to thank include Alex Avdichuk, Brian Barnes, Stuart Beaton, Audrey Borges, Tobi Bruce, Jennifer Cheney, Jil Courtice, Michael, Cullen, Paul Duvall, Janet Cousins Ewan, Anne Goddard, Miriam Harris, Sonya Herring, Heather Home, Anna Hudson, John Kettle, Stephen McCanse, Gordon McNamara, Joan Murray, Roald Nasgaard, Daniel Payne, Janice Passafiume, Dr. Bernie Ross, Simonette Seon-Milette and David Taylor. A special thanks to Claire Dawson and Fidel Peña for the sensitivity with which they have designed this publication.

To the private collectors across Canada who so willingly shared their work and opened their homes, as well as the public galleries, I am particularly indebted. Thank you for making this exhibition possible.

The Robert McLaughlin Gallery staff is truly a team in the most positive sense of the word. Thank you, in particular to David Aurandt, Barb Duff, Robert Roch and Olexander Wlasenko.

Finally, for sharing our library floor and desk with mounds of books for a two and a half year period, I thank Mark, Spencer and Ethan.

Linda Jansma
Curator

INTRODUCTION

Rody Kenny Courtice can be seen as one of Canada's "forgotten women." The exhibition and this catalogue seek to redress the exclusion and examine Courtice's contribution to the lexicon of Canadian art history.

In her thesis on the exclusion of artists Alexandra Luke and Hortense Gordon from the canon of art history, Janice Anderson argues that this exclusion is partly due to the fact that in order to address gender inequality, "the understanding of how women work within the matrix of culture, but outside the discourse which selects what will remain as the written record of that matrix, demands that issues of gender discrimination be addressed."[1] She goes on to say that within the patriarchal structure, there is a public/private dichotomy in which women "function equally intrinsically in the private," while men function in the public sphere.[2]

Anderson is correct in asserting that there is a fear of relegating female artists to the "private" sphere by examining their personal lives. However, I feel that Courtice's private life contributed greatly to her practice. Therefore, before the business of her art is actually dealt with, I will give readers a picture of who Courtice was as an individual.

Included in this catalogue is a selection of letters that Courtice wrote to Isabel McLaughlin, as well as a few to A.Y. Jackson and other artist friends. These letters, under the heading "Greetings!!", an oft-used salutation by Courtice, are glimpses into her personal life and how that life fit into the whole of her artistic career.

Also included is a comprehensive Exhibition History. Courtice was particularly active in society exhibitions, but also showed her work in solo, two-person and group exhibitions. This listing is important not only in tracking work, but also in dating and titling work. I am grateful to Mary Helms, a Gallery summer student in 2004, for assisting in compiling this list.

---

1 Janice Anderson, *Closed Systems: Alexandra Luke, Hortense Gordon and the Canadian Art History Canon* (Concordia University: Québec, Thesis in the Department of Art History, September, 1995), 16.
2 ibid, p. 17.

CHAPTER I

A ROSE
BY ANY OTHER
NAME

Picturesque, Creative, Energetic, Pure Magic, Small, Dark, Resourceful, Inventive, Witty, Adaptable. These are only a few of the terms used to describe the woman variously known as Rose, Roselin, Roselyn, Rosalind and finally Rody Kenny Courtice.

Her Irish great grandfather, Hugh McGonigal, eloped with Scottish Margaret Maclachlan around 1828, arriving in Ontario where they purchased 3,000 acres of land and went into the timber business. This property would eventually be sold and the Parliament Buildings constructed on the site.[1] Mary, one of Hugh's and Margaret's four children, married Christopher Tierney and located to Arnprior or Renfrew in the Ottawa Valley. The third of their eleven children, Margaret, married Bernard Carroll Kenny and settled in Renfrew. They had four children: Mona, Rose, Tony and Walter.

On her paternal side, Courtice's grandparents were John Kenny and Elizabeth Carroll. While little is known of the Kenny family, it is known that Elizabeth was the granddaughter of William Carroll, who was loyal to the British Crown and moved from the United States to work on the Rideau Canal.[2] Mona Kenny Cannon, Courtice's sister, would recall that her younger sister was very much like her grandmother Elizabeth in both character and wit. Rody Kenny was born on August 30, 1891,[3] and it was her father Bernard, a tile mason,[4] from whom Mona felt Courtice inherited her artistic talents: "Rody was interested only in drawing and painting, even at that early age. In this she was papa's girl because he was a very good sculptor. He did some beautiful things in marble."[5]

Courtice's early years are sketchy: what is known is that she attended a convent school in Renfrew and completed four years of high school.[6] Mona recalls trips to a cabin built by their father in Haliburton where they would skinny-dip and Courtice would pose and declare: "Renoir would love us," due to, as Mona explained, "a few bulges we had."[7]

A bridesmaid for her sister and Bill Cannon in 1912, Courtice followed them west, arriving in Calgary in the summer of 1913. Besides joining a tennis club with her sister, she was "constantly in demand...accepting invitations from numerous admirers." Mona continues: "It was wonderful to have Rody with us. She was witty and adaptable, and always in a good humour. She was the perfect kind of young woman for a dynamic West."[8] She stayed on in Calgary until the spring of 1914.

Returning to Toronto, Courtice found that many of the men she had known had joined up to fight in the Great War and had either left for overseas or were still in training. Like many of her friends, she took a Volunteer Aid Department course and continued to be asked to "many parties where the boys in uniform and in training were present."[9] She eventually met, and married soon after, Henry Lloyd Hammond, a member of the Royal Flying Corps (which would become the Royal Air Force on April 1, 1918). Shortly after their November 5, 1917, wedding, they left for Dallas, Texas where Lloyd Hammond was posted to train Americans. Courtice "often flew with him in the front open cockpit of the bi-wing aircraft as he flew under bridges and barn-stormed the surrounding farm land."[10] After their return to Toronto and Hammond's posting overseas, Courtice joined the no. 4 School of Aeronautics at Victoria College, a group that her sister was also a member of. There they wrote orders of the day and kept records. "I think it was August 4th, 1918, when the cable came from the War Office. All it said was: 'missing, presumed dead.' I saw Rody shrivel with horror, and sorrow."[11]

A little over a month after the news of her husband's death, Courtice was plunged into Toronto's Spanish Flu epidemic that arrived from Europe with Canada's returning soldiers. Toronto's medical officer of health, Dr. Charles Hastings, likened the epidemic to a "cyclone" and reported that the final tally of dead in the city was 1,750[12] (up to 40 million world-wide). Due to the number of medical staff who became ill with the disease, many women, including Courtice, answered the call for volunteer Sisters of Service (SOS). She probably received the three hours of training offered to volunteers, along with a blue and white satin SOS badge.[13] Mona Kenny Cannon recalls that Courtice was one of the first to volunteer her services, working with a family of four in North

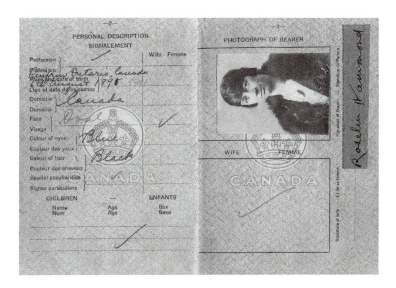

Toronto while also helping Mona who was so ill with the disease that she could barely walk. "Her trilling laughter was stilled, but there was about her an inner strength which was noticeable. She was a heroine without a doubt, and, I, among others owed her my life."[14]

In the fall of 1920, as a mature student, Rody Kenny Hammond began studies at the Ontario College of Art.

---

1 Letter from Mona Kenny Cannon to Paul Courtice, October 27, 1977.
2 op. cit., Cannon; letter from Paul Courtice to Linda Jansma, October 26, 2004.
3 On all National Gallery of Canada artist information forms, dating from 1942, and a 1946 information form for *Who's Who in American Art*, Courtice lists her birth date as August 30, 1895. A passport from 1924 clearly shows, in the area of date of birth, a "5" in 1895 that has been crossed out with pencil and replaced with a "1"; 1891, in pencil, is repeated beside the ink date. Her gravestone in Port Perry, Ontario, also states her year of birth as 1891.
4 "Our papa was born on the same day which must have explained why he thought Rody was the brightest member of our family." Letter from Mona Kenny Cannon to Paul Courtice, August 20, 1977.
5 Letter from Mona Kenny Cannon to Paul Courtice, August 12, 1980.
6 *Who's Who in American Art*, Questionnaire, received August 14, 1946 (on file in RMG artist file).
7 Letter from Mona Kenny Cannon to Paul Courtice, December 14, 1976.
8 Letter from Mona Kenny Cannon to Paul Courtice, August 1, 1977.
9 Letter from Mona Kenny Cannon to Paul Courtice, March 14, 1978.
10 E-mail from Paul Courtice to Linda Jansma, April 19, 2002.
11 Letter from Mona Kenny Cannon to Paul Courtice, March 14, 1978.
12 Interestingly, it was in Courtice's hometown of Renfrew that one of the worst outbreaks of the disease was reported on October 4, 1918. Louisa Taylor and Kirsty Duncan, "The Great Flu Pandemic," *Toronto Star*, (October 30, 2005), A10-11.
13 ibid, A11.
14 Letter from Mona Kenny Cannon to Paul Courtice, March 14, 1978.

CHAPTER 2

ONTARIO
COLLEGE OF ART
AND BEYOND

The Ontario College of Art began its life as the Ontario School of Art in 1876. In 1912 it was incorporated as the Ontario College of Art (OCA), after also being the Toronto Art School and Central Ontario School of Art and Industrial Design. On September 30, 1921, the college opened its own building (designed by Principal G.A. Reid); it was the first building of its kind in Canada to be dedicated solely to the education of professional artists.[1]

Courtice entered the college in the fall of 1920 when G.A. Reid was principal and Arthur Lismer was vice-principal. In the 1920-21 prospectus, the teaching staff included J.W. Beatty, Emanuel Hahn, R. Holmes, Arthur Lismer, C.M. Manley and G.A. Reid as instructors, and Yvonne McKague and Edyth Coombes as assistant instructors. In her first year of instruction at the college, it was recorded that Rosalind Hammond received a first year certificate in elementary class; the following year, Roselin Hammond received an honorable mention in design in Mr. MacDonald's class; in 1922-23 she received a donated scholarship in applied design, third and fourth year; and in her final year, 1924-25, Roselin Hammond received a diploma of general proficiency and post graduate scholarship.[2]

Her life-long friendship with Yvonne McKague (later Yvonne McKague Housser) began with their relationship as teacher and student. Housser began teaching at the college shortly after she had been graduated in 1918 but would remember that "I hardly taught her [Courtice] because she was really a contemporary but I did a little bit." Housser not only used the term "contemporary" to describe Courtice's age relation to her, but also used the term to describe the woman herself, saying that "She was contemporary…an interesting woman and quite individual."[3] It was Housser who introduced Courtice to the industrial towns of Northern Ontario such as Gowganda and Cobalt and who continually supported her through reviews, letters and even with an initial attempt to support her application to membership of the Royal Canadian Academy.[4] Doris McCarthy recalled the relationship between Housser and Courtice: "…she [Housser] and Rody Kenny Courtice used to go down the corridors of the College of Art laughing and those two women both had the most contagious laughs. …oh, it was wonderful to hear them. You could hear them all over the school. …Rody was small and dark and compact… and the two of them made an amusing contrast as they walked around the College."[5]

Lismer, who arrived at the college in 1919, reformed art education in the school despite the conservative leadership of G.A. Reid. He would eventually resign his position in 1927, frustrated with the establishment. While there, he made a definite mark on how his students were taught: Mary McKay recalled that "he [Lismer] was an inspiration. I remember him saying 'Look for five minutes and paint for one.'"[6] Isabel McLaughlin, another close friend of Courtice's, said of Lismer: "He had some dead leaves, people would call them dead, but they were all the most interesting shapes and he said 'not to just regard the thing as a dead leaf. Look at the form.' He said, 'You can see mountains in them, all sorts of things and you know, small objects can, with imagination, become anything.'"[7]

Mrs. Roselyn Hammond is first listed as assistant librarian of the college in its 1923-24 prospectus. No reference to another librarian was found during this time, so one can assume that Courtice was solely responsible for librarian duties.[8] She also acted as assistant instructor during the years until her resignation in 1927, including teaching at the college's Port Hope summer school that was begun in 1923 in a mill that the college had purchased. The 1924-25 prospectus describes the summer programme:

> …A resident instructor and assistants conduct an excellent course in
> Drawing and Painting from landscape. Outdoor Figure and Animal
> Study, etc. A dining room and dormitories – a large tent outside for
> the men students, and a magnificent studio with north light…Board
> and accommodation is very reasonable – about $7.50 per week.[9]

In 1924, Courtice, under the name Roselin Hammond, traveled through Europe on bicycle with fellow artists Kathleen Daly (who was also attending

OCA at the time) and Yvonne McKague. There is one known painting from these travels. Entitled *St.-Jean-De-Luz, Basses – Pyrenees, France*, it depicts a figure making its way up a curved street in the French seaside town close to the Spanish border. The lampstand on the left and tree on the right precariously frame the composition, while the red-roofed houses serve to constrict the street into mid-ground. The paint strokes on this small panel show an assured use of the oil medium and a strong colour sense, with areas of red leading the eye throughout the composition.

Her passport from this extended trip was stamped in London, Paris, Venice and Milan. While in Europe, she attended croquis classes at the Grande Chaumière in Paris and also observed art classes in London. It is interesting to note her take on a European education. In a letter dated May 7, 1948, to a Mrs. McQuillan (and copied to Isabel McLaughlin) regarding an upcoming September article in *Chatelaine* magazine on the *4 Women Who Paint* exhibition, Courtice writes:

> It is always my contention when speaking to groups or persons concerning art education, that while experience in any school can be helpful, it is not essential to have attended schools abroad. I therefore, wondered if the paragraph commencing something like this "All have studied in Europe"…might contain the following information concerning me:

> Mrs. Courtice was not registered in any school but painted and sketched with other students in London, Paris, Venice and Milan, etc., attending croquis classes in several schools.[10]

Courtice's assertion is that an all-Canadian arts education is as relevant as one that includes diplomas from European institutions. Her loyalty towards OCA, considered one of Canada's pre-eminent centres for arts education at the time, is obvious. She, along with the Group of Seven before her, makes claim for a strong national identity, one that includes a strong educational system.

On August 14, 1926, Courtice married Andrew Roy Courtice in Chicago at Saint James Chapel. In the *OCA Student's Annual* of May, 1927 it is noted:

> Mrs. Hammond – now Mrs. Roy Courtice – is living in Chicago – at least she was up to a short time ago – but life is uncertain – in Chicago. The corridors still echo with her energetic heel and toe clack as she chases recalcitrant student holders of books from the library. 'Hammy' is remembered with affection.[11]

St. James Chapel, Chicago
1926

The Courtices lived in Chicago where Roy worked as a lawyer, at least until the end of 1930.[12] While in Chicago, Courtice took courses at the Art Institute of Chicago, studying the figure under Karl Buehr and puppetry with Tony Sarg at the institute's Goodman Theatre.

Mona McCardle, Roy's niece, recalls with fondness the Courtices' relationship:

> 'They are a great pair.' – a silly phrase but conveys to me the aliveness of their relationship. ...their diverging pursuits and accomplishments in business and art kept a mutual respect and admiration and disinterest (meaning interested but not involved) alive in their marriage. Rody could be very intense and Roy was her tempering influence ...Roy enjoyed Rody's creativity, verve and energy. He was her solid base.[13]

Roy Courtice's support of Courtice's artistic career can be seen to stem from his relationship with his mother. Ada Mary Brown was an early twentieth-century suffragette married to Andrew Courtice, a Methodist pastor. She was widowed at an early age, and went on to found the Home and School movement, open her own school (the Balmy Beach College) and become a "vocal exponent of the advancement of women."[14]

With Roy's sister, the Courtices originally purchased a five acre property on the Scarborough Bluffs called Cory Cliff. In 1933 they sold the property to Rosa and Herbert Clark who owned the adjacent forty acres and would create there The Guild of All Arts. Interestingly, Clark purchased a selection of paintings by Courtice in 1980 that would eventually be housed as part of the Guild collection.

In 1935 Roy and Rody Courtice purchased an 1850 stone house (with twenty-five acres) in Markham. The stone out-building, which had housed tractors, trucks and cars, became Courtice's studio after large double doors were replaced with windows (while Rody Kenny Courtice was unconvinced of the wisdom of purchasing the property, it was Roy who pointed out the possibility of a studio in the second stone building).[15]

Paul recalled:

With mother so occupied, oft preoccupied with art, we had a maid, who had come from a neighbouring farm. She lived with us winter and summer, and cooked great farm food.[16]

In the winters the Courtices rented a furnished flat in Toronto, as the farm was not only difficult to access, but also hard to heat. In the early years they lived in a three-storey apartment building at 90 Balsam Avenue with Roy's sister and her family living in the flat below (the building being owned by both Roy and his sister). They also lived on Elm Avenue and in the Frontenac Arms on Jarvis Street.[17] Paul remembers this latter location with fondness due to its reputation as the city's red light district.[18]

While many of Courtice's works exist in public and private collections throughout Canada, there are far fewer than she produced. Her niece, Joan Penney, recalls the artist burning a stack of paintings before they sold their Markham property in the early 1960s. This is confirmed by the artist's son who recalls, as a young child, his mother dragging many paintings to the flagstone patio between the house and her studio at their Markham property, and setting them ablaze. Paul felt that there may have been as many as one hundred early works destroyed in the mid 1930s. He remembers his mother being "depressed for days" after the burning, and that life with Rody was unpredictable: "she could be a warm, loving mother one moment and desperately frustrated the next moment."[19]

Other surviving works by Courtice from this period are etchings and aquatints. Two aquatints from 1925 depict houses in Toronto's Ward district – plain, somewhat decrepit buildings that recall Lawren Harris's series of paintings from a few years earlier. There is, in Courtice's work, a certain animation in the animals she would depict in later works, but also seen in the buildings found in both prints and paintings. One untitled print shows a house in the evening, the lit window casting an enormous beam of light across a third of the composition; this exaggerated beam serves as an abstracted beacon from the house into the world.

The Educator

Courtice's teaching career did not end with her time at the Ontario College of Art. She taught throughout the 1930s with Arthur Lismer and his innovative Saturday morning children's programme at the Art Gallery of Toronto (approximately 600 children a year, aged seven to fourteen, would take advantage of the free three-hour classes[20]). This programme, under the influence of Viennese child art educator Franz Cizek, encouraged giving the "imaginative capacity of the children free reign."[21] One of Courtice's fellow teachers recalled:

> We all had a gallery full of boys and girls, anywhere between 50 and 80, with one teacher and two assistants. None of us wanted to teach the 13 year old group because they were so lethargic…Rody knew what to do. She just put her hand in her pocket, brought out a whistle, and BLEW it. They all sat up and got to work again, but a whistle resounds throughout a building like a spacious Art Gallery, and so, in all the rooms, everyone sat up and got to work again.[22]

Courtice, ever interested in progressive ways of teaching, also taught art to teachers in summer courses, as well as teaching children in her studio in Markham. She notes that she gave lectures with such titles as: "Munsell Colour System" and "Art Experience for Children Using Discarded Materials." Writing in *Chatelaine* about the *4 Women Who Paint* exhibition, Thelma LeCocq comments on Courtice's ability to recycle material on hand to produce work: "...[Courtice] is the most resourceful and inventive of the four in the way of using materials on hand for creative art. 'Show her a garbage can,' they say, 'and she can produce a mural.'"[23]

In 1936, Lismer traveled to Africa on a Carnegie Foundation grant permitting him to organize a system of art training for children. After his return to Canada he sent one of the Art Gallery of Toronto teachers, Norah McCullough, to continue the work in South Africa. In a letter to A.Y. Jackson, Courtice writes:

> ...when you mentioned Norah going to Africa as Mr. Lismer's assistant, you know Mr. Lismer offered that job to me first. It was a difficult decision to make but I turned it down and recommended Norah – I often wonder where I would have ended up if I had accepted.[24]

Unlike her single friends Yvonne McKague Housser and Isabel McLaughlin, Courtice's obligations to family did affect her career. Towards the end of her life she stated: "It's very difficult to successfully combine the roles of wife, mother, and artist, but if you fight hard enough you can do it."[25] While exhibition opportunities were numerous and Courtice writes "I don't think that I have been discriminated against [as a woman] by either the public, critics, or juries,"[26] within the confines of her role as educator there is a certain amount of resentment: "I have never felt that A.L. [Arthur Lismer] gave Norah, or Audrey, or in fact any of us, credit (in his "September Gale") for the loyal support we gave him during that time at the Gallery – certainly we got no adequate financial reward."[27]

1 undated, untitled article, 1920, from Ontario College of Art and Design (OCAD) Archives in the Dorothy H. Hoover Library; www.ocad.ca/about_ocad/history.htm.

2 *Ontario College of Art Prospectus*, 1920-25, Ontario College of Art and Design Archives in the Dorothy H. Hoover Library; *Globe and Mail* (May 16, 1921); *Globe and Mail* (May 14, 1923); *Globe and Mail* (May 16, 1925).

3 Interview, Joan Murray and Yvonne McKague Housser, June 24, 1985, The Robert McLaughlin Gallery archives.

4 "Those so and so's of R.A.'s didn't elect Rody. Probably I was wrong one to put her up, I don't think I am their dearest pet." Letter from Yvonne McKague Housser to Isabel McLaughlin, October 1, 1953; copy in The Robert McLaughlin Gallery archives.

5 Interview, Joan Murray and Doris McCarthy, March 29, 1992, The Robert McLaughlin Gallery archives.

6 Interview, Joan Murray and Mary McKay, December 15, 1982, The Robert McLaughlin Gallery archives.

7 Interview, Joan Murray and Isabel McLaughlin, December 17, 1982, The Robert McLaughlin Gallery archives.

8 E-mail from Daniel Payne, Head, Reference, Information and Access Services, Dorothy H. Hoover Library, OCAD, to Linda Jansma, October 19, 2005; Pearl McCarthy noted that in her position as assistant librarian, Courtice had been "turned loose to buy, collate, catalogue and guard the library." Pearl McCarthy, "Galaxy of Talent in Four Artists," *Globe and Mail* (July 5, 1947), 9.

9 *Ontario College of Art Prospectus*, 1920-25, Ontario College of Art and Design Archives, Dorothy H. Hoover Library.

10 Copy of letter from Rody Kenny Courtice to Mrs. McQuillan, Queen's University Archives: Coll. 2303.37, Box 6, File 15, 1933-1964.

11 *The OCA Students' Annual*, (May, 1927), 27.

12 Paul Courtice, who was born on June 15, 1931, writes that "I was conceived in Chicago but born in Toronto." E-mail from Paul Courtice to Linda Jansma, October 27, 2004.

13 Mona McCardle, "Auntie Rody." I am grateful to Karen McCardle for providing me with a copy of this tribute to Courtice.

14 Terry Crowley, "Ada Mary Brown Courtice: Pacifist, Feminist and Educational Reformer in Early Twentieth-Century Canada," *Studies in History and Politics*, vol. I, no. I, (Fall, 1980), 97.

15 Paul Courtice, "Growing Up With Rody," 2004, 1-2.

16 Courtice, 3.

17 In a letter to Isabel McLaughlin, dated June 29, 1953, Courtice explained that she and Roy had purchased a house on Glenhowan Road: "I had thought all along that I wanted a house in the city so we could eliminate all this moving… but I feel now I'd rather be back in an apartment." Queen's University Archives: Coll. 2303.37, Box 6, File 18, 1941-1953.

18 Courtice, 2.

19 Interview, Linda Jansma and Joan Penney, May 15, 2006; interview, Linda Jansma and Paul Courtice, November 29, 2005.

20 Arthur Lismer, *Education Through Art for Children and Adults at the Art Gallery of Toronto* (Toronto: Art Gallery of Toronto, 1936).

21 John A.B. McLeish, *September Gale: A Study of Arthur Lismer of the Group of Seven* (Toronto: J.M. Dent & Sons, 1955), 124.

22 Erma Lennox Sutcliffe, *Rody Kenny Courtice: A vignette*, Archives of Ontario, F1182, MU 8092, File: Biographies "C": Toronto Heliconian Club Papers, 1975.

23 Thelma LeCocq, "4 Women Who Paint," *Chatelaine*, vol. 21 no. 9 (September, 1948), 9.

24 Letter from Rody Kenny Courtice to A.Y. Jackson, February 23, 1959, Archives of Canada, MG: M630D351; File 24; Volume 91.

25 *Eclectic Eve*, J. Cameron, ed., [et al.] (Toronto: Canadian Women's Education Press, [1974?]), unpaginated.

26 ibid.

27 op. cit. letter from Rody Kenny Courtice to A.Y. Jackson.

CHAPTER 3

THE GROUP
AND ITS
INFLUENCE

As the popular version of the Group of Seven's history would have it, J.E.H. MacDonald wrote to A.Y. Jackson in Montréal about "the belief of some of the younger Toronto artists that it was time Canadian painters relied less on European traditions and began to paint our own country as it was."[1] As for their subject matter: "it was above all in nature that Harris and the other future members of the Group would base their optimistic beliefs for Canada."[2] F.B. Housser, who published the first book on the Group in 1926, effusively writes:

> The north is here – its incomparable sunlight; its whiffs of balsam, pine and spruce; front-touched corners of the forest; the splash of tumbling rapids and cub water-falls. The land is beginning to talk. The studio windows are shuttered up and cobwebs hang on the slats. Something is being born. The tang of the north is colouring souls as it colours the leaves in autumn.[3]

This romantic notion of a Canadian art movement has been challenged on numerous fronts. Lynda Jessup asserts:

> ...the Group's work and activities articulated an exclusive national identity based on an Anglo-Celtic ancestry, exclusive on the one hand of indigenous peoples, certainly, and on the other of the immigrant.

For Ontario viewers, the landscape in paintings by the Group of Seven was not a place of productive labour, nor a permanent home, but rather a place of recreation – of scenic value and spiritual renewal.[4]

Courtice was immersed in the Group of Seven's philosophy of an art for a nation since its inception in 1920. She entered the Ontario College of Art in the same year that the Seven had its first exhibition at the Art Gallery of Toronto, and would, of course, have been taught by its members, as well as being a colleague of some of them while she worked at the college. She wrote to A.Y. Jackson in 1959:

> I started at the Ontario College of Art in the fall term of 1920, when it was still in the old Model School. I soon became acquainted with all your names and was very aware of what was going on, through listening to Mr. Lismer when he would come back from the Arts & Letters Club after having had lunch listening to Hector Charlesworth, etc. And later, in the second year when I was put on the staff I was privileged to gather at breaks, in the corner studio, when we got a lot of backwash of what the Group was doing. It was a thrilling time for you Seven – it was even thrilling for us just to be in the atmosphere of what you were doing.[5]

This appreciation of being on the periphery of the "inner circle" is further illustrated in a 1966 letter to Jackson in which she speaks of a recently published book by Blodwen Davies and recalls that in a personal copy of an earlier Davies book, the author had written: "For Rody who also shared the effort and the dream of Tom Thomson."[6] Yet this seeming adulation is less obvious when Courtice is dealing with her close friends. In her essay, Lynda Jessup writes of the Group of Seven landscape tradition "in which artists created views of outlying regions for consumption by this [central Canadian] metropolitan market."[7] This could not be more literally true than in the anecdote that Yvonne McKague Housser tells of a sketching trip to the north shore of Lake Superior that she and Rody had made. It is worth quoting in full:

> It was now getting well into September and sketching outdoors was chilly. Rody Courtice had joined us. She and I decided to climb up through the forest to a rocky open place where we could see the lake beyond the thickly wooded area. The sky was a dull grey backdrop and we were not inspired. After trying several sketchbook

compositions with no enthusiasm we started to pack up and give up for the day. As Rody put her things together she found a tiny bottle of gin in her paintbox. We drank it, then Rody had an inspiration and said, 'Let's build a still life, a Lawren Harris.' We dragged a dead, bare small tree trunk and some branches onto the bare rock and propped them up with logs and rocks that were lying near us. We made quite an interesting composition and as a few snowflakes came drifting down we opened up our paintboxes and set to work with shamefaced amusement and enthusiasm. We worked hard and fast and though cold we were rather pleased with ourselves; the day had not been entirely wasted.

Both of us did large canvases from these bogus sketches and when I last spoke to Rody just before she died I said, 'That was pretty disgraceful wasn't it?' She smiled and said, 'And worse still we sold them.'[8]

Courtice's niece, Joan Penney, recalls Roy Courtice asking Courtice "why can't you do that?" referring to a Lawren Harris iceberg painting, "So she did," said Penney, "and hung it beside the door in their apartment."[9]

Despite these gentle digs at the increasing legend surrounding the Seven throughout the end of the 1920s and into the 1930s, Courtice created paintings that can easily be placed within the lexicon of modernism advanced by the Group. Indeed, her work was considered worthy enough for inclusion in the Group's 1931 exhibition. While derivative of the Group's style, Courtice's early work is accomplished; she was a gifted and highly skilled colourist and had a particularly adept sense of composition. The sketch for *March Sunlight, Baie St. Paul* shows a house behind trees and their shadows that reach across the entire panel. The snow rises from the foreground and is intercepted by an undulating picket fence that continues into the hills in the background ("only those who have painted in snow know what a special thrill it can be," she wrote to A.Y. Jackson[10]). In the larger canvas of the same name, Courtice has moved the horse and carriage to a more prominent foreground location and positioned the house further back and to the left in the composition. The mound of snow in the foreground is more prominent as are the blue shadows of the trees that stretch across it. The picket fence now dances its way through the hills while the sky ascends from the horizon line in a light green/blue to a darker shade at the top of the canvas.

The faceless, hooded figures in *St. Fidele, P.Q.*, who come toward the viewer in horse and buggy, are far less animated than the muddy, undulating

A Group of Friends at Whitefish Falls
(Courtice pictured front row, second from right)
1936

road and askew hydro poles that are replicated in the crosses that stand atop the church in the background. The sunlight strikes the side of the buildings, leaving them awash in pink and yellow. The sketch for the work (entitled *Sunday Morning, Baie-St.-Paul*) has an even more highly keyed colour scheme, with a brighter palette throughout. There are other canvases and board paintings of quaint villages nestled among hills that are of a kind, all bearing Courtice's practiced and skilful hand.

In describing Tom Thomson's *Jack Pine*, Fred Housser muses: "One could believe that this tree was to the nature-worshipper Thomson what the symbol of the cross was to a mediæval mystic."[11] Not unlike her mild snub of the Seven with the constructed Harris on Lake Superior, Courtice, in 1929 and 1930, created a series of works on the same theme, the lowly sumach taking the role of the majestic, single wind-blown tree so often found in paintings by Tom Thomson and the Group and given elevated symbolic significance by Housser. In a linocut, sketch and canvas of *Sumachs – Lake Superior*, Courtice leads our eye from the lower portion of the composition with massive boulders that burst through the Canadian Shield. The sketch on board has its boulders boldly outlined in black, flattening them into coloured masses, unlike the painting where the boulders are specific, three-dimensional masses. In each work, the sumach is cut off by the top of the composition, pushing it out from the confines of the rectangular support and not giving it the majesty found in the central tree images by Group members. The uppermost sumach reaches double branches

to the side of a central, twisted trunk, a crooked neck giving form to a precarious bird ready for flight. This work expresses a vision that would become uniquely Courtice's by the mid-1930s.

Yvonne McKague Housser was on the scene of the industrial north sooner than most, making her initial trip to Gowganda in 1917. Courtice was one of the first of her friends whom she invited on subsequent trips. "...At the end of the war, my former hostess loaned me her cabin so Rody Courtice and I took off to Gowganda, changed trains at Cobalt for Elk Lake... Rody was a great person on a sketching trip, inventive and fun. When life was difficult she would say, 'Remember Yvonne, we are here for our health.'"[12] One of Courtice's most accomplished paintings from this period is *A Northern Railway Town* in the collection of the Art Gallery of Hamilton. In a valley, surrounded by hills in the background, is nestled the small town of Schreiber.[13] The railway winds into the centre, and beyond it are the smoking stacks of its roundhouse. The town has little to recommend it – no trees, parks or life beyond the railway. And Courtice does little to romanticize the place – however, the majestic scale and handling of the paint brings a particular dignity to its subject. Alicia Boutilier notes that the "deliberately rudimentary" way in which Courtice paints the houses and train assisted her to "convey her own view of Lake Superior country."[14] An earlier panel, *Cobalt Silver Mine*, also shows a town from above, but this one a view that is more amongst the buildings and more tightly framed. The buildings are props around which Courtice lays down snow in ranges of whites, blues and mauves, while her customary askew hydro poles cast twisting shadows. There is a stateliness in this mélange of buildings, calling to mind the town's noble history as a primary northern mining community.

In a print entitled *Coniagas Mine: Shafts in Snow* published in the December, 1939 issue of *Canadian Forum*, the forms of the three mine shafts are once again simplified – standing starkly against a snow-riddled sky. The three shafts dominate the landscape, towering over three small figures working their way down a narrow path. The diagonal snow peppers the entire composition with its unifying jabs, making clear the harsh conditions in which many of the Northern Ontario residents lived. This is not a pristine landscape devoid of either people or the impact that they have made on the land. Rosemary Donegan, in her exhibition catalogue *Industrial Images*, writes of this subject matter:

> The shapes of the mine-shafts, each unique against the northern
> sky, the isolation of daily life, and the strength of light, were to cap-
> ture the imagination of such artists as A.Y. Jackson, Rody Courtice,
> Franklin Carmichael, and Isabel McLaughlin.[15]

In *Near Chalk River* from 1933, Courtice again paints a valley surrounded by rolling hills, this time with a meandering river running through it. This landscape contains a single home surrounded by worked land, a fence delineating the boundaries of ownership. This toy house seems somewhat ridiculous against the solidity of the hills – something easily pushed into the water below. The light blue river snakes through the composition, gently nudging the shore and leading beyond and behind the range of hills. No longer is Courtice emulating a particular Group style in these works; there is a strength of vision that is further refined in later work.

1 A.Y. Jackson, *A Painter's Country: The Autobiography of A.Y. Jackson* (Toronto: Clarke, Irwin & Company Ltd., 1958), 21.
2 Charles Hill, *The Group of Seven: Art for a Nation* (Ottawa: National Gallery of Canada, 1995), 22.
3 F.B. Housser, *A Canadian Art Movement: The Story of the Group of Seven* (Toronto: The McMillan Company of Canada, Ltd., 1926), 49.
4 Lynda Jessup, "The Group of Seven and the Tourist Landscape in Western Canada, or The More Things Change…," *Printemps*, Vol. 37, Issue 1, (Spring, 2002), 145, 146.
5 Letter from Rody Kenny Courtice to A.Y. Jackson, February 5, 1959, National Archives Canada, MG: M630D351; File 24, Volume 91.
6 Letter from Rody Kenny Courtice to A.Y. Jackson, October 20, 1966, National Archives Canada, MG: M630D351; File 26; Volume 82.
7 Jessup, 152.
8 Yvonne McKague Housser, "North Shore of Lake Superior," *Northward Journal*, no. 16, (1980), 29.
9 Interview, Linda Jansma and Joan Penney, May, 2004.
10 Letter from Rody Kenny Courtice to A.Y. Jackson, June 21, 1966, National Archives Canada MG: M630D351; File 26; Volume 82.
11 F.B. Housser, 120-121.
12 Yvonne McKague Housser, "Mining Country," *Northward Journal*, no. 16, (1980), 24.
13 In an undated poem, Isabel McLaughlin writes of a trip with Courtice to Schreiber:

Rody

I came north with three ladies, one gent,
On painting the scenery intent
Meals made by one Paul
Filled abdominal wall
Left a bulge where there once was a dent.

On the north shores of Superior
We drank water with bacterior,
Ate chickens from the coop
Talked to ladies with a whoop,
Growing wearier, and wearier and wearier.

The Robert McLaughlin Gallery archives.

14 Alicia Boutilier in *Lasting Impressions: Celebrated Works from the Art Gallery of Hamilton*, ed. Tobi Bruce (Hamilton: Art Gallery of Hamilton, 2005), 138.
15 Rosemary Donegan, *Industrial Images* (Hamilton: Art Gallery of Hamilton, 1987), 70.

CHAPTER 4

AN
INDIVIDUAL
VISION

Courtice's move to an individual artistic vision can be likened to the transformation of Georgia O'Keefe, who said:

> I realized that I had a lot of things in my head that others didn't have... I decided to start anew – to strip away what I had been taught – to accept as true my own thinking.[1]

Asked to describe her own work, Courtice wrote:

> I feel that no one element or ingredient in painting can be described as the drive to creative work; and that the integrated whole, being the reflection of emotional, intellectual and aesthetic reactions, becomes too involved to catalogue. I do feel, however that change being the very basis of our life, the creative artist will be the articulation of the pattern of his times. If I am asked if I am a naturalistic painter I would say 'yes.' If I am asked if I am an abstract painter I would say 'yes.' I feel each work I undertake has a personality of its own conditioned by the urge that prompted that work. I am accused of being a humorous painter, but I do not consciously say 'I am going to paint a humorous picture.' If it is humorous, it grows as I paint.[2]

Art historian Paul Duvall, who remembers Courtice as a teacher at the Art Gallery of Toronto when he was a student there, describes Courtice's unique style as opposed to the "strident air in the work" of the 1930s and 1940s. He felt that there was a particular lightness in her work that could be characterized as "a painter who enjoyed painting."[3] Critic Pearl McCarthy also recognized the singularity of Courtice's vision: "There was a time when some critics thought Yvonne McKague Housser and Rody Kenny Courtice might prove mere variations on a theme from the old Group of Seven. The friendship to the old Group remains, but these artists are not like anybody but themselves now."[4]

For much of her career, Courtice painted larger canvases in her Markham studio, begun as studies in the fields around their property, while in winter the trend was towards smaller paintings that could be managed in her more confined quarters in Toronto. There is a whimsy in these works, but nothing that takes away from their quality as paintings. Paul as a young boy is surrounded by massive leaves in *A.P.K.C (Paul C)*, his overalls staying in place with only one strap. The design element of Courtice's work is never in doubt: the blue and green leaves are boldly outlined, the figure placed slightly left of centre and framed within the composition by two crossed branches. There are few remaining portraits done by Courtice (if, indeed, she produced many at all). Figures in her works are often stylized as seen in *Tobacco, St. Thomas, Potato Pickers' Rhythm, Ontario Sugar Cane* and *Portuguese Fisher Women*. Oblivious of the artist, the people continue their work – bent over a field of potatoes, steering a box of tobacco, hauling buckets into a farmhouse, cleaning and sorting the day's catch. It is that rhythm of daily work that Courtice captures in her canvases – imbuing each figure with both dignity and grace. While the figures seem caught in a moment, the settings in which they are placed are alive with movement, particularly seen in *Potato Picker's Rhythm* and *Ontario Sugar Cane*. The trees in the former canvas, bearing their fall colours and in Van Gogh fashion, sway around and behind the figures who seem oblivious to their dance while the sugar cane bows towards the receding figure. Yvonne McKague Housser was astute in her analysis of her friend's work when she wrote: "Rody Kenny Courtice paints rural Ontario in a way that conveys a feeling for both the country and the people."[5]

Where Courtice particularly excelled, however, was in her depiction of animals. In describing an illustration of *Just Cows* in *Canadian Home and Gardens*, the caption writer unfortunately states: "A modern composition with highly recognizable figures – a jolly piece of work by one of Toronto's women artists."[6] While Courtice felt her exhibition opportunities were equal to her male counterparts it is statements like these, albeit in a magazine focused on women's interests, that assist in relegating women to a position outside the canon of art history, outside of the need for serious analysis.

Just Cows is one of Courtice's larger remaining canvases and shows six Jersey cows (or perhaps the same cow in six positions), lying throughout the composition. Some are sleeping, one looks to the side, while yet another looks towards the viewer. Overlapping these massive forms are Cezannesque plains making broken space that highlights each cow individually. A similar treatment is seen in *My Cat*, although the plains are predominantly relegated to the background, so that just a few areas of the lush-foliaged surroundings tip onto the cat's white body. The feline is moving, alert, animated and shows the personality known by her owner. Another composition favouring cats is *July Siesta*. Three cats are centred in a verdant backdrop of leaves and greenery. The cats are an odd shade of terracotta – leaving an impression of figurines rather than the living, breathing animal in *My Cat*. *Country Pattern* shows a grey horse, legs somewhat unnaturally splayed in the centre of a composition of rolling hills. A wooden fence bars the front of the canvas, the horse behind it spreading its legs over recently emerging plants. Conical trees lead the eye into the background of the painting, surrounding a barn and silo. Of her painting *The Pet Rooster*, Pearl McCarthy writes: "Rody Kenny Courtice has the most beguiling candor and joy of life in every brush stroke."[7] A child sits in a loft, rooster under her arm, looking out over the country side that includes both a house and windmill. Two almost toy-like, undersized chickens are at her feet, feet that are glowing an otherworldly blue while her rooster sits contentedly under the girl's "wing." Part of the composition is framed by timbers that make up the barn – giving the whole a theatricality that definitely leans towards the comic.

The most accomplished painting in this series of canvases is *The White Calf*. This image would be Courtice's contribution to the silkscreen project instigated by the National Gallery of Canada, and spearheaded by A.Y. Jackson and A.J. Casson, to distribute reasonably priced images of Canadian art to schools and offices. The project was originally begun to help decorate soldiers' barracks in World War II with Sampson-Matthews Limited of Toronto responsible for their printing. A single white calf stands in the middle of the painting surrounded by sumachs and mullein stalks. As the sumach organically spreads its branches to form the back of the composition, the mullein, in turn, stands at attention around the front of the canvas, surrounding the calf (would Courtice have known that the mullein was believed to have magical powers to ward off wild beasts and other dangers?). The colours include rich golds and reds, while the light grey of the calf punctuates the centre of the painting. The calf is standing on a circular path, calmly engaging the viewer, almost encouraging us to follow. There is something particularly spiritual about this image: a white calf perhaps instead of the white lamb found in Christianity; the circular path denoting a never-ending circle – the conjoining of the beginning and the end. Courtice spent over twenty-five years in the midst of animals and fields at her Markham home, longing, as her son Paul writes, "for something more expansive."[8]

While wintering in her Toronto home, Courtice constructed still lifes that included her son's and other's toys. *Nella's Horse*, a watercolour, depicts a pull-toy skillfully painted in a highly designed background of dramatic yellow and black zigzags with the ubiquitous conical trees in the background that she used in her paintings set in the country. *Boy's Window* shows tiny tin soldiers guarding two large pots of cyclamens. In this work, Courtice employs a treatment similar to the composition in *Just Cows*: the work is overlaid with prismatic plains that dissect the space into cubist blocks. Paul Duvall describes *The Silly Ass* as revealing Courtice's "keen sense of the ridiculous in poetic terms."[9] Interestingly, Duvall argues that the mid-century move away from landscape painting to figurative work with subjects of wit, pure humor and satire would be what assisted Canadians "groping for national adulthood."[10] *The Silly Ass* is one of Courtice's most fantastic and strange paintings. It shows a toy ass sitting on its end among seven pots of hyacinths. Behind it are seven hooded, haloed figures standing in a blue-lined tunnel. The flowers and the figures are opposites: as the hyacinths are ready to burst out in bloom, the figures are gathered in on themselves, closed to the world. The ass is witness to all of this, chuckling at the absurdity of his surroundings – the jester in the court. One can speculate that Courtice is commenting on the closed rituals of the church in which she was raised, versus the freedom found in a nature without rules. What *is* certain is, as Duvall notes, the "poetic terms" in which she carries out this work. The disparate elements of tiny figures with large potted plants and a toy ass in a somewhat otherworldly setting combine to create an intriguing painting that generates more questions than it answers.

In a review of the *4 Women Who Paint* exhibition, Thelma LeCocq noted the few works that were "tinged with social consciousness."[11] and was likely referring to work by Courtice. This exhibition includes two paintings by Courtice that are particularly politically based. *Dove's Dismay*, purchased by the Art Gallery of Toronto in 1944, shows two doves watching a scene of war through a barred window with a soldier on a horse, another walking off a cliff, planes shooting through the sky with a parachuting figure falling to the water below. The scene is one of pandemonium and chaos and was surely spawned by Courtice's memories of her first husband's death when his plane was shot down over the English Channel. Although Courtice supported the war effort through her involvement with the Heliconian Club and participation in the Art Gallery of Toronto's poster contest (for which she won second prize for her print *Nurses are Needed*), she is on the side of the pacifist doves who are witness,

as we are when viewing this work, to war's ultimate madness. The Cold War is evoked in *The Game* from circa 1949. In it, Courtice shows a chess board with two large knights representing the opposing factions, the USSR's sickle prominently displayed on the board and emblematic of that nation while a chess piece with a Christian cross symbolizes the West. After living through two world wars, Courtice reduces conflict to a deadly game.

The Scene

"The art community in Toronto was certainly a closely knit one. Everyone knew everyone else and often the same individuals served on different committees 'working for the arts.'"[12] Courtice was certainly a part of the Toronto arts community. Paul Courtice writes that his mother's day "was a whirlwind of activity… morning at the Toronto Art Gallery [sic] for a picture hanging, early afternoon painting out a sketch at her easel in her Bathurst-Street studio, then preparing for a skit at Toronto's Heliconian Club in the late afternoon. That would have been a typical RKC day."[13]

Besides participating in numerous exhibitions each year, Courtice was a member of the Heliconian Club (a woman's arts and letters club established in Toronto in 1908), serving as its president from 1932-33; a member of the Canadian Society of Graphic Arts, the Ontario Society of Artists, the Canadian Society of Painters in Water Colour, the Canadian Group of Painters, serving on its board in 1945, 1947/48 and again in 1954/55, the Federation of Canadian Artists, serving as the president of the Ontario region in 1945/46 and was a member of the Royal Canadian Academy. She attended the historically significant Kingston Conference in 1941, which emphasised the artist's role in society and which led to the establishment of the Federation of Canadian Artists.

More important than Courtice's involvement in various societies and clubs was her connection with fellow artists, particularly women artists. Of Courtice, Isabel McLaughlin, Yvonne McKague Housser and Bobs Haworth it was written during the time of their four-person exhibition at T. Eaton Gallery in Toronto:

> They're women who enjoy each other's [sic] company because they have a common interest. Except when they go on holidays together, they never paint together. Each has her own studio, her own style of painting. Each respects the other's work, and what is more remarkable, they are able to accept each other's criticism in a spirit of helpfulness and with no resentment.[14]

It is with these women that Courtice could be most honest, as is obvious from her correspondence with McLaughlin. In these letters she shares her opinions on art, her gratitude for being included in various art excursions, her frustration at times with caring for sick family members. These women were extremely encouraging of each other as is evident in a letter from Yvonne McKague Housser written to Courtice, McLaughlin and Prudence Heward when the three women were on a sketching trip together: "...all three of you are, (and have in your work) a real Canadian quality, individual and fine – so go after it..."[15] Although friends with Arthur Lismer, A.Y. Jackson, Charles Comfort, Gordon MacNamara and other male artists, Courtice only exhibited in smaller group exhibitions with other female artists. Was this due to choice or lack of opportunity? Was this lack of visibility with her male counterparts part of the reason behind Courtice's lack of visibility in contemporary accounts of Canadian art history?

---

1 Mara R. Witzling, ed., *Voicing Our Visions: Writings by Women Artists* (New York: Universe, 1991), 6, as cited in Elizabeth Martin and Vivian Meyer, *Female Gazes* (Second Story Press, 1997).

2 *Who's Who In Ontario Art*, (August, 1952), 190.

3 Interview, Linda Jansma and Paul Duvall, November 1, 2005.

4 Pearl McCarthy, "Four Artists Strengthen Ontario Art," *The Globe and Mail*, Toronto, (March 20, 1948).

5 Yvonne McKague Housser, "Canadian Group of Painters – 1944," *Canadian Art*, vol. 1, no. 4 (April – May, 1944), 145.

6 *Canadian Home and Gardens*, 16, (April, 1939), 61.

7 McCarthy.

8 Courtice, 1.

9 Paul Duvall, "Self-Satirization in Canadian Art Suggests This Nation Is Finally Attaining Adulthood," *Saturday Night*, 63, no. 4, (September 27, 1947), 2.

10 Duvall, 2.

11 LeCocq, 107.

12 Christine Boyanoski, *The 1940s: A Decade of Painting in Ontario* (Toronto: Art Gallery of Ontario, 1984), 8.

13 Courtice, 1.

14 LeCocq, 8; for a thorough analysis of the exhibition *4 Women Who Paint*, as well as the relationship between the artists, see Alicia Boutilier, *4 Women Who Painted in the 1930s and 1940s* (Ottawa: Carleton University Art Gallery, 1998).

15 Letter from Yvonne McKague Housser to Isabel McLaughlin, Prudence Heward and Rody Kenny Courtice, October 20, 1944; copy in The Robert McLaughlin Gallery archives.

CHAPTER 5

THE
LATER WORKS

In 1949, Robert Ayre wrote an article in *Canadian Art* on the history of the Canadian Group of Painters from its inception in 1933. He discussed the first exhibition held in November of that year in which landscape continued to hold sway, although Bertram Brooker presented works that were the only abstractions. In 1942, Ayre continued, there was a resurgence of work that dealt with "the urgent human issues of the war." He noted, however, that "Rody Kenny Courtice called her canvas *War* but it was a pure abstraction."[1] In dealing with the 1949 submissions by the Group, Ayre again mentioned that Courtice's offering, *Memento Mori*, was part of a group of paintings that he labeled "the purer abstract."[2]

Although the painting *War* has not been discovered, it is interesting that Courtice was working in an abstract vein as early as 1942. She would have been one the earliest Canadian women artists to do so.[3] In her 1952 *Who's Who in Ontario Art* submission, she noted: "I do feel, however that change being the very basis of our life, the creative artist will be the articulation of the pattern of his times."[4] Until the end of her career, Courtice continued to stretch her artistic vision to reflect the art world around her.

Courtice's paintings from the 1950s and 1960s show a push away from what people saw as her "humorous" paintings, to work concentrating more completely on form and colour. *Butternut and Pears* and *Dish of Pears*, both circa 1950, are small still lifes; the bowls are outlined, Matisse fashion, in black and placed in box settings. These boxes are tilted panels of colour with, in the case of *Butternut and Pears*, no illusion of three-dimensionality. Another work from this period, *"Fish Hawkers" Cape Cod* shows three men, arms outstretched with that day's catch. Courtice combines the figures with various seaside effects: starfish, buoys, seaweed and nets. Overall she has joined these elements with transparent waves of green and blue creating an impression of Cape Cod rather than an exact replication of the seaside area.

German-born painter Hans Hofmann, opened his first summer art school in Provincetown in 1935. Joe Plaskett, in an article about Canadian artists who studied with the abstract expressionist painter, noted:

> The intellectual demands Hofmann makes on his students are enormous. They must painfully break down preconceptions and learn to command what is almost a mystical science of creation, which, however, is not guided by rule or logic, but by "empathy" or a "feeling into."[5]

Courtice joined Isabel McLaughlin and Alexandra Luke in Hofmann's 1950 summer session in Provincetown, Massachussets. McLaughlin would recall that Hofmann's classes were "such a different thing," and that the artist himself was "terribly inspiring." She also recalled that Hofmann would tear apart his student's drawings only to reassemble them in order to achieve a new composition.[6] Of his famous "push and pull" theory, Hofmann wrote:

> To create the phenomenon of *push and pull* on a flat surface, one has to understand that by nature the picture plane reacts automatically in the opposite direction to the stimulus received... *Push* answers with *pull* and *pull* with *push*...the same thing can happen to the picture plane in a spiritual sense.[7]

In a letter to McLaughlin shortly after their return from Provincetown, Courtice writes: "I am still chewing on 'push and pull' and 'too much verticality,' etc., etc.,"[8] That she not only "chewed" on her lessons, but applied them, can be seen in works such as *Canal Composition* and *Flight*. The first work is a series of geometric shapes, the black being pushed back to accommodate the pull of the white, the yellow holding the compositional elements together. In *Flight*, a series of wing-like shapes overlap each other, dark again, contrasting with light, lending the forms an elegant sense of movement. As with the work *War*, referred to by Robert Ayre, Courtice seemed unwilling to abandon the natural world, making reference to it in her titles. *Prairie Wind* is one of her larger abstractions – a whirling mass of red and white paint with gold leaf, as well as

areas of white inscribed and scratched into the surface of the painting. The title immediately suggests rolling tumbleweed, while birds are referenced in *Flight* and shapes of ships and sails in *Canal Composition*.

In 1952, Courtice's work was included in the first nationally based Canadian exhibition of abstract painting organized by Alexandra Luke (although the "nationality" of the exhibition is somewhat in question as only one of the invited Québec artists, Leon Bellefleur, submitted work). The *Canadian Abstract Art Exhibition* traveled from the Oshawa Y.W.C.A., where it originated, to galleries in Ontario, New Brunswick and Montréal. That Courtice was invited to submit two works for inclusion in the exhibition shows the respect with which her work, within the abstract idiom, was held.

Courtice did not limit her experimentation to pure abstraction. *Crows, Weather Birds* and *Sea Horse Ballet* are swirling compositions that multiply a specific icon, be it birds or sea creatures. In these paintings she has pushed her earlier format from the late 1930s and 1940s, of cows, cats or horses that dominate the landscape, to one in which the animals or birds act as just another element within the composition. As her sketching trips continued, so too did Courtice's

allegiance to the land. Later paintings such as *Uxbridge Country, St. Lit des Capes* and *Country Gothic* show a continued affinity for landscape painting. As Courtice says: "I feel each work I undertake has a personality of its own conditioned by the urge that prompted that work."[9]

> Art today is experimental to the vanishing point, but that kind of an upheaval I think is very productive of some real painting, and some real art. There's no way of knowing the future of art; art will find its level just like water.[10]

Rody Kenny Courtice said these words shortly before her death, on December 6, 1973, of cancer. At 82 she had witnessed monumental change in Canadian art, understanding that change was instrumental to producing what she termed "real art." She boldly came "out from behind the Canadian Shield"[11] as Paraskeva Clark, with whom she exhibited, challenged and encouraged Canadian painters to do – into a vision that was uniquely her own in the late 1930s and 1940s. Her strengths undoubtedly lay in depicting what she intimately knew – the country side around her Markham home and smaller vistas that she created within her Toronto apartment. As a mature artist, she continued to push, learning the vocabulary of abstraction much earlier than many Canadian artists, and applying it to works that became part of an abstract lexicon that began with Bertram Brooker in the 1920s. A 1934 portrait of Courtice by Dorothy Stevens shows Courtice sitting cross-legged in the grass (hardly what would be considered a proper pose, but certainly reflective of her character). She wears a black dress with a large black pendant necklace hanging heavily around her neck. Hair pulled back, an uneven line of black bangs frames a serene face. Behind her is the family's Markham home – its stone house on the left and studio building on the right. Roy, her husband, leans against a fence, while Paul, her son, runs through the yard. This is a portrait of the artist in the fullest sense – a portrait of Courtice would seem incomplete without this setting. This independent-minded woman added an exemplary body of work to the canon of Canadian art history; her contributions are worth remembering.

---

1 Robert Ayre, "The Canadian Group of Painters," *Canadian Art*, vol. vi, no. 3 (Spring, 1949), 99.

2 ibid, 101.

3 Other women who worked in an abstract idiom from an earlier time are Kathleen Munn, Edna Taçon and Marian Scott.

4 *Who's Who In Ontario Art*, (August, 1952), 190.

5 Joe Plaskett, "Some New Canadian Painters and Their Debt to Hans Hofmann," *Canadian Art*, vol. x, no. 2 (Winter, 1953), 62.

6 Interview, Joan Murray and Isabel McLaughlin, October 21, 1979, The Robert McLaughlin Gallery archives.

7 Hans Hofmann, "The Search for the Real in Visual Arts," ed. Sara T. Weeks and Bartlett H. Hayes Jr., *Search for the Real: Hans Hofmann* (Cambridge: MIT Press, 1948/1967), 44.

8 Letter from Rody Kenny Courtice to Isabel McLaughlin, July 28, 1950, Queen's University Archives: Coll. 2303.37, Box 6, File 15, 1933-1964.

9 op. cit., *Who's Who In Ontario Art*.

10 op. cit., *Eclectic Eve*.

11 Paraskeva Clarke [sic], "Come out from behind the Canadian Shield," *New Frontier*, vol. I, no. 12 (April, 1937), 16-17.

PLATES

St.-Jean-De-Luz Basses – Pyrenees, France c. 1924

OIL ON BOARD, 21.3 X 26.3 CM
COLLECTION OF KAREN MCCARDLE

Sunday Morning – Baie St. Paul c. 1929

OIL ON CANVAS, 41.1 X 51.3 CM
ONTARIO HERITAGE TRUST, AN AGENCY OF
THE GOVERNMENT OF ONTARIO

Early Morning, Rossport, Lake Superior 1930

MEZZOTINT ON PAPER, 11 X 12 CM
RAIN COLLECTION

Sunday Morning Baie-St.-Paul c. 1929

OIL ON BOARD, 21.6 X 27 CM
RAIN COLLECTION

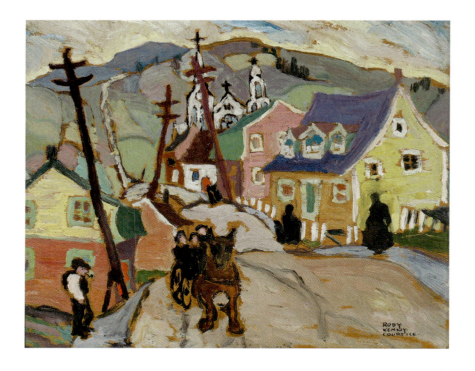

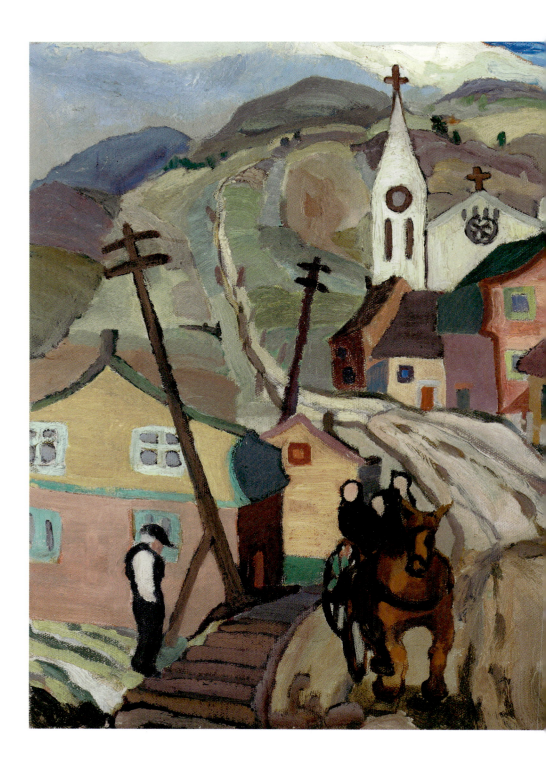

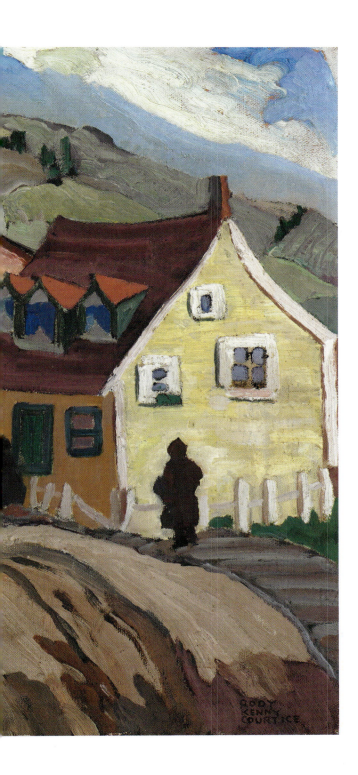

St. Fidele, P.Q. c. 1930

OIL ON CANVAS, 41.1 X 51.2 CM
ONTARIO HERITAGE TRUST, AN AGENCY OF
THE GOVERNMENT OF ONTARIO

Sumach, Lake Superior 1929 (RIGHT, ABOVE)

LINOLEUM PRINT ON PAPER
14.7 X 15.3 CM (PAPER); 12 X 14.1 CM (IMAGE)
COLLECTION OF KAREN MCCARDLE

Sumachs – Lake Superior C. 1930 (RIGHT, BELOW)

OIL ON PRESSED BOARD, 30.4 X 35.3 CM
ONTARIO HERITAGE TRUST, AN AGENCY OF
THE GOVERNMENT OF ONTARIO

Sumachs – Lake Superior C. 1930 (BELOW)

OIL ON CANVAS, 86.5 X 102 CM
ONTARIO HERITAGE TRUST, AN AGENCY OF
THE GOVERNMENT OF ONTARIO

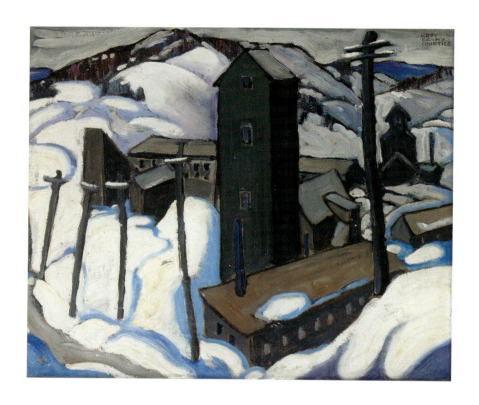

Cobalt Silver Mine c. 1930-35

OIL ON BOARD, 30.5 X 35.6 CM
PRIVATE COLLECTION

Near Chalk River, Ontario 1933

OIL ON CANVAS, 86.5 X 101.9 CM
PRIVATE COLLECTION

March Sunlight, Baie St. Paul c. 1935

OIL ON CANVAS, 61.0 X 71.2 CM
ONTARIO HERITAGE TRUST, AN AGENCY OF
THE GOVERNMENT OF ONTARIO

Bog Orchids, Lake Simcoe c. 1936

OIL ON CANVAS, 61.0 X 45.7 CM
COLLECTION OF CARL
AND TRUDY MICHAILOFF

Nella's Horse c. 1936

WATERCOLOUR ON PAPER, 26 X 30 CM
PRIVATE COLLECTION, CALGARY

Tobacco – St. Thomas, Ont. c. 1935

OIL ON CANVAS, 86.5 X 101.5 CM
PRIVATE COLLECTION

Portrait of Mona n.d.

OIL ON CANVAS, 40.5 X 30.2 CM
PAUL COURTICE BESTOWAL COLLECTION TO
THE ROBERT MCLAUGHLIN GALLERY

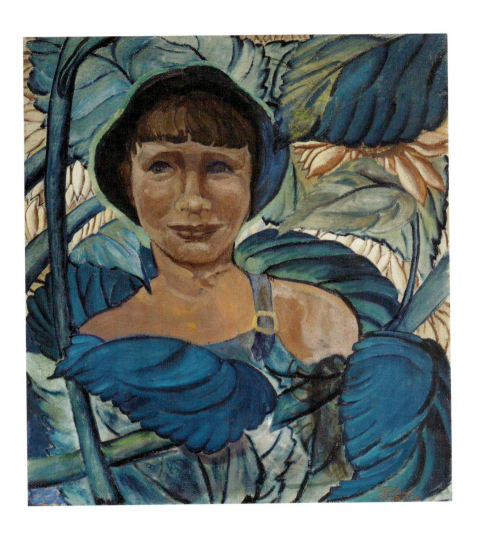

A.P.K.C. (Paul C.) c. 1937

OIL ON CANVAS, 53.5 X 46 CM
PAUL COURTICE BESTOWAL COLLECTION TO
THE ROBERT MCLAUGHLIN GALLERY

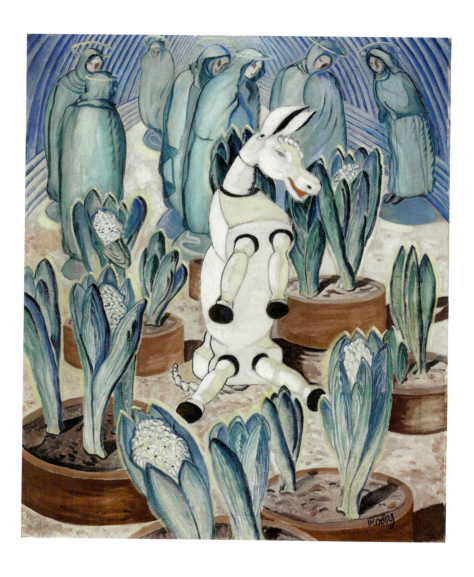

The Silly Ass c. 1937

OIL ON CANVAS, 77.5 x 62.2 CM
PRIVATE COLLECTION

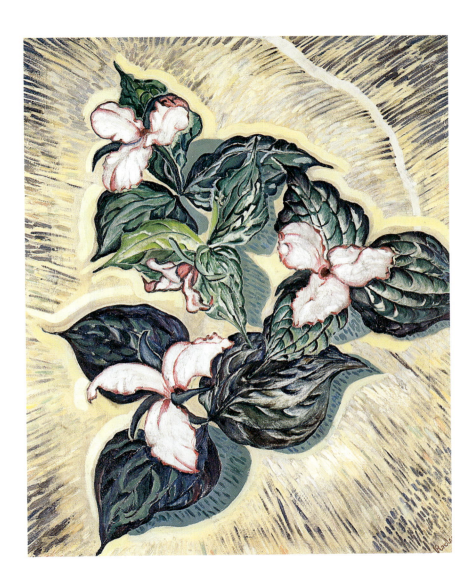

Fading Trilliums c. 1938

OIL ON CANVAS, 30.5 X 24 CM
PRIVATE COLLECTION, CALGARY

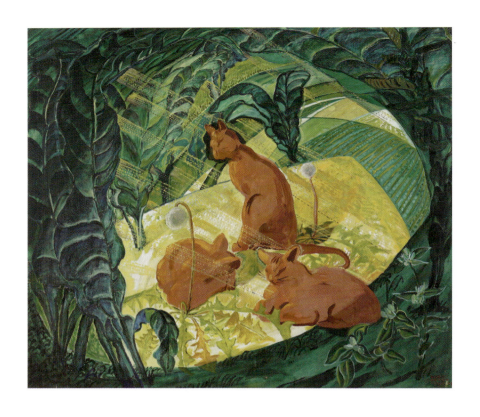

July Siesta c. 1938

OIL ON CANVAS, 110 X 122.5 CM
COLLECTION OF
TÉRÈSE TÉMOIN DOWNS

Just Cows c. 1939

OIL ON CANVAS, 91.4 X 99 CM
COLLECTION
OF JIL COURTICE

November Pickings c. 1939

OIL ON CANVAS, 40.5 X 50.7 CM
PRIVATE COLLECTION

Potato Pickers' Rhythm C. 1939

OIL ON CANVAS, 40.5 X 50.5 CM
PRIVATE COLLECTION

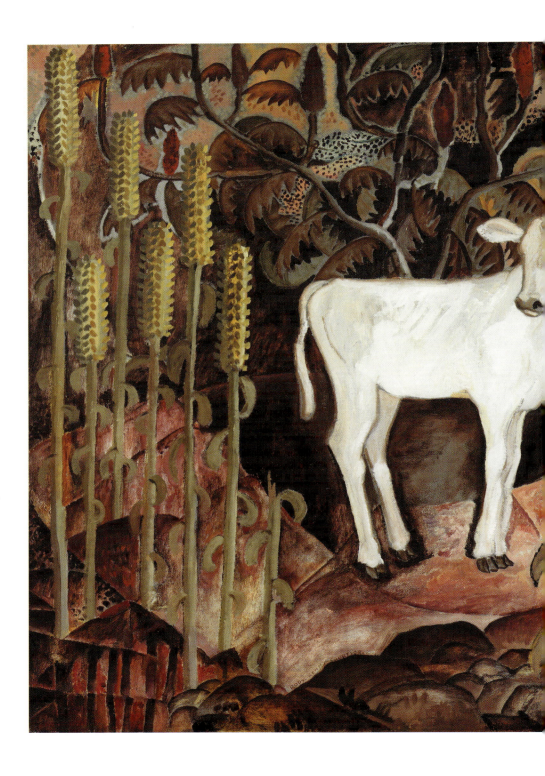

The White Calf c. 1941

OIL ON CANVAS, 72.5 X 87.5 CM
COLLECTION
OF KAREN MCCARDLE

Country Pattern c. 1940

OIL ON CANVAS, 85 X 70 CM
PRIVATE COLLECTION, CALGARY

Country Church – Quebec c. 1945

OIL ON PANEL, 30.2 X 35.2 CM
COLLECTION
OF DIANE WILLEMSE

Boy's Window c. 1942

OIL ON CANVAS, 60 x 60 CM
CANADIAN FINE ARTS GALLERY,
TORONTO

Doves' Dismay 1944

EGG TEMPERA ON PANEL, 35.4 X 40.6 CM
ART GALLERY OF ONTARIO;
PURCHASE, 1944

Parable of the Pigeons 1947

OIL ON CANVAS, 58.4 X 53.3 CM
HART HOUSE, UNIVERSITY OF TORONTO,
PERMANENT COLLECTION

My Cat c. 1948

OIL ON CANVAS, 58 X 74 CM
THE ROBERT MCLAUGHLIN GALLERY;
PURCHASE, 2003

"Fish Hawkers" Cape Cod c. 1951

OIL ON BOARD, 85 X 100 CM
PRIVATE COLLECTION, CALGARY

The Pet Rooster c. 1948

OIL ON MASONITE, 40 X 34.5 CM
PRIVATE COLLECTION, CALGARY

Butternut and Pears c. 1950

OIL ON CANVAS, 27.6 x 37.1 CM
PRIVATE COLLECTION

Flight c. 1953

OIL ON MASONITE, 70.9 X 50.6 CM
PAUL COURTICE BESTOWAL COLLECTION TO
THE ROBERT MCLAUGHLIN GALLERY

Sea Horse Ballet c. 1955

Canal Composition c. 1962

WATERCOLOUR ON PAPER LAID DOWN
ON MASONITE, 46 X 53.7 CM
PAUL COURTICE BESTOWAL COLLECTION TO
THE ROBERT MCLAUGHLIN GALLERY

Prairie Wind c. 1963

GOLD LEAF AND EGG TEMPERA
ON MASONITE, 102 X 87.1 CM
PAUL COURTICE BESTOWAL COLLECTION TO
THE ROBERT MCLAUGHLIN GALLERY

Weather Birds c. 1966

WATERCOLOUR ON PAPER LAID DOWN
ON MASONITE, 40.5 X 30.9 CM
PAUL COURTICE BESTOWAL COLLECTION TO
THE ROBERT MCLAUGHLIN GALLERY

Dorothy Stevens, Canadian, 1888-1966
Conversation Piece of Rody Kenny Courtice c. 1935

OIL ON CANVAS, 109.2 x 86.5 CM
VARLEY ART GALLERY / TOWN OF MARKHAM

GREETINGS!!

Dear Isobel…[sic]

While I lay in bed at the hospital and received such lovely flowers, I composed very fitting replies – but ah me!! They were never written. Yours (I can't think of the name of them were the first I had of that kind and their orange was a real middle value "Munsell" complementary for the blue with them.

You were kind to remember me when I know you have so many things to do.

Our invitation to you for Friday was very informal but so is the occasion – it's hard to be formal with a bambino.

Till Friday
Rody.
K.
C.

Cory Cliff
Scarboro
Aug 12 – 1931

QUEEN'S UNIVERSITY ARCHIVES: COLL. 2303.37, BOX 6, FILE 19, 1944-1966

Dear Isabel

I think your show was grand – I was glad I waited and saw it properly – the variety of subject[s] you have is amazing – you must have gotten a big thrill out of seeing your "children" all hung and making such a successful debut. Large congratulations.

And Roy and I offer our appreciation of being included in your dinner-party. We loved it – and I'm taking good care of my lowers.

Sincerely
Rody

Toronto/Feb/15/33

QUEEN'S UNIVERSITY ARCHIVES: COLL. 2303.37, BOX 6, FILE 15, 1933-1964

HART HOUSE THEATRE is endeavouring, during the coming season, to take advantage of its splendid facilities for the promotion of a real Little Theatre and I feel sure the attached programme will interest you.

RODY. KENNY. COURTICE

Member of the Special Committee

[LETTER INCLUDED A SUBSCRIPTION FORM FOR THE HART HOUSE THEATRE 1935-1936 SEASON]
POST MARK JULY 8, 1935
QUEEN'S UNIVERSITY ARCHIVES: COLL. 2303.37, BOX 6, FILE 17, 1939-1969

Dear I.G.

It's Monday morn – and I do hope this will get there before you leave – I'm sending it anyway.

There was certainly a lack at Balmoral on Friday having dinner there – it was you that was missing – however we had a lovely dinner, then went to water. C. show and then to "Gala Hel. Night." We only got there for the last third of the programme, which was very good – and it was well attended – so I think everybody was satisfied.

We expected to move to the country Apr. 1 – but it is still too juicy – but remember if you yearn to send me a picture postcard of any Bermuda growth or bird (for my picture coll. for the country school children – the address R.R. 1 – Markham is always good.

In this year of our Lord – 1939 – on the 3rd day of April being the birthday of my lord Roy – we both send our love and xxxxxxxxx and Paul xxx

Best regards to Mrs. McLaughlin.

POST MARK APRIL 3, 1939
QUEEN'S UNIVERSITY ARCHIVES: COLL. 2303.37, BOX 6, FILE 17, 1939-1969

Dear Isabel,

    …Nella says there is an ante room to an officers' mess in Camp Borden badly in need of murals – that some of the officers saw Newmarket and would the Hel. Club consider doing it – I asked when and Nella said, possibly for "Kent's" visit (that['s] how democratic we are getting) and I said I did not think it could be done by then. Myself, I think we should ask them for subject matter suggestions – to be treated soberly or jocosely or what – told Nella you would be returning sometime after the 20 Aug. could she wait – also told her that you had paid for paints used at Newmarket and I thought the War Fund should handle it – she agreed but thought the decorations should be signed "I.G. McLaughlin"
    "Heliconian Club"
Or   "Rody Jones Corset"
    Heliconian Club etc.
    And "as the Hel. reputation was at stake it should be done properly" so she would try and make them wait. Isn't the underlined Nellish and I wondered if some of the "Hunting-print" devotees from Newmart [sic] had been speaking to her – the ones I mean who thought a few choice hunting scenes would have been more suitable than our efforts.
    …Lightning hit our studio on the N.E. corner knocked out the wooden gable end – split some beams, knocked down plaster and sent a splinter through the canvas I was working on – it took me a long time to get roused to starting that canvas and now I must start over, and its tough going.
    …I wish you were here for a couple of hours to discuss this constitution re. Kingston Conference. They want the completed questionnaire by Aug. 9.

…Missing you and best
Roy
Paul
Rody

R.R. 1
Markham
Aug. 1 – 1941

QUEEN'S UNIVERSITY ARCHIVES: COLL. 2303.37, BOX 6, FILE 18, 1941-1953

Dear Isabel: Greetings, Welcome to Pres. of C.G.P.
ditto " " "   Hel. Club

re ANY FURTHER MURALS FOR SOLDIER HOUSING

As Grace Craig will be telling you soon, things finally came to a head at
Newmarket in what Grace calls, soothingly, a carousal, and some of the murals
were torn off the walls or wrecked in some way. She is very disturbed about K.
Pepper's because apparently being near the bar it got the worst blast and is no
more, and neither is mine above ground, etc, etc, etc. Some one of the men
also said "These women must have been drunk when they did these murals".
Apparently between the two factions, for and against the decorations, there
was a big point as to where the authority had come from, for the decoration
of the walls and that apparently Col. Harkness could do nothing because there
had been no proper authority given to us, a kind of "Wouldn't-it-be-nice-to-do-
the walls" suggestion.

THEREFORE, BE IT RESOLVED BY US, that we be very careful about
any future ventures. Nella says that an officer who saw the Newmarket ones
made very complimentary remarks about them. GRACE SUGGESTED THAT
WE NOT TELL ANYONE OUTSIDE OURSELVES ABOUT NEWMARKET,
SO NELLA DOES NOT KNOW THERE WAS ANY UNPLEASANTNESS.
I suggested to Nella that when the proper authority was given they should also
suggest some material for the type of decoration they want. Conservative
mediocrity, no doubt.

This is not meant to dictate to you, Pres., but merely to state the position
as it is to date.

XXXXX   RODY   XXXXX

POST MARK AUGUST 29, 1941
QUEEN'S UNIVERSITY ARCHIVES: COLL. 2303.37, BOX 6, FILE 18, 1941-1953

Dear Isabel

You are not more THRI!!ED than I am that I have been asked to go with you – it is just the right time and I, too, feel the urge to "art" in both discussion and actually… Your "own inimitable handwriting" is wonderful, just like you, hardly any mistakes and any that there are, are characterful.

Your asking me for assistance in menus is droll, when I think of the food I always get at "Chez Isabel". However, from my experience in getting meals three times a day for weeks on end, I can give you something of what I find, for me, is economical in time and effort. I used to scorn what I think I recall Miss Birioukova terming "the foundation of meal preparation", – the weekly roast. I now rely on it as a stay against uneasiness of "what to have for dinner".

…I am enclosing a questionnaire and envelope (to save your time). I have Maida coming on the 9th, to take charge for two weeks, I hope, so everything looks rosy, or Rody.

Rody

Isabel:

Questionaire

Are you taking a long dinner dress

Is it alright to take an electrical heating pad?

If I wanted to treat a small canvas with hot gelatine and dope, would it be convenient for me to use a stove –

…Have you read "Silly Girl" Angna Enters autobiography and did you think her comments on painting worth discussing? [Angna Enters was an American pioneer in mime, a dancer, an author, teacher, painter, and sculptor.]

To be answered to the best of your ability and may God have mercy on your soul.

Love – Rody

POST MARK OCTOBER 2, 1944
QUEEN'S UNIVERSITY ARCHIVES: COLL. 2303.37, BOX 6, FILE 19, 1944-1966

Dear Prue [Prudence Heward]:

...I have been thinking about that corrugated on which our murals were to be done. I think that the cracks where the fibre has been folded show because the corrugated cell has been broken down and that it would show a smooth surface if all the cells were broken down – I mean if that mural of mine were laid face down on a clean surface and something rolled over it so that all the corrugations were flattened it would give a smooth front and at the same time might cure that te[n]dency to curve out at the top from the wall. If you rolled it out before you started to use it, the paint would not collect in the crack and make a streak particularly in Isabel's case if she is going to use show card. It is just an idea. Laid on the garage floor with a lawn roller rolled over it, being sure there is no grit under it which would poke through.

I hope your model came and that she was interesting – the trouble is that "life is too short".

It was nice seeing you again, love
Rody

Frontenac Arms, 306 Jarvis St.
Toronto, Oct. 26' 1944

QUEEN'S UNIVERSITY ARCHIVES: COLL. 2303.37, BOX 6, FILE 19, 1944-1966

Dear Isabel

And so ends a most pleasant week, in a delightful spot and with a most efficient hostess...

I hope I didn't cause too much row getting out yesterday morning – I came away in a glowing state of mind and body, owing to Elsa's taking the responsibility of getting me up and having breakfast ready for me – it was like night outside and very strange getting on a train at that hour – I quite enjoyed the sensation – felt I was on the steppes in Russia or fleeing the "Nasties".

I came home to find the family practically hospital cases – Roy had been running a temp. up to 104 since Monday, Dr. Curtin calling twice a day – has an infected throat (having planted 12 poplar trees in the country on Sunday in the rain), ... Paul making a touch in soccer, was kicked with a spiked boot on the ankle, they tell me it swelled so you wouldn't know he had an ankle – had an X-ray with a surgeon all ready for what I hate to think, as they were afraid it was osteomylitis (? spelling) – thankfully the X-ray showed it was only the soft tissues affected so they handled that nicely although it still looks infected to me.

So I feel as if I had been stretched in forty different ways.

Fancy writing a thank-you letter on the typewriter and telling you all the woes.

But one other reason I am sending this off immediately is that I wanted to say that Maida says the stores in which we buy, have the canned things I coveted in Cowansville, apparently the new packs are making it possible. So in case you seriously meant you were going to express asparagus, corn, etc. I wanted to save you any trouble.

The train (pool at 3.p.m.) From Montreal was crowded with service men and their wives – my good deed for the day was minding a two-weeks old baby of a service man's wife, travelling alone, while she went to the toilet and to the diner – it (the baby) was so small I was afraid each time it might stop breathing while she was away.

All my thanks, Isabel for giving me a nice holiday, love
Rody

Frontenac Arms,
306 Jarvis st.
Toronto, oct 26′1944

P.S. – Roy although a little shaky send[s] his love.

QUEEN'S UNIVERSITY ARCHIVES: COLL. 2303.37, BOX 6, FILE 15, 1933-1964

Dear Isabel

You seem to have been away a long time – I've missed you.

We were very intrigued being mixed up with the navy and we loved the bottle – very clever isn't it? Thanks so much

I supposed you have come back just bursting to draw nudes next Wednesday at 2 pm.

Love and best wishes for a year that brings peace, with victory.

Sincerely
Rody

Toronto
Jan 3 – 1945

QUEEN'S UNIVERSITY ARCHIVES: COLL. 2303.37, BOX 6, FILE 15, 1933-1964

Dear Isabel

Crash! bang – !! tinkle, twinkle!!!
twinkle! little! trillium, bang!!!!
bang ding dong –

This is all a sounding of cymbals for the indefatigable President of the C.G.P. – You organized and produced it most wonderfully and I know whereof I speak because I watched the painstaking care of one Izzy.

Your party afterward was very, very enjoyable, speaking with aesthetic and gustatory appreciation, to say nothing of the notables present.

The attendance at the gallery was most stimulating I thought – had an aura somewhat of a new explosive feeling that I used to feel at the early Group of Seven shows.

In helping with the labels on Friday I kept wondering when I was going to get a label for a certain canvas to which I was attracted – finally I unhooked the canvas and it was your "Twinkle" – I was also fooled by one of Yvonne's and one of Peter's.

I hope you are taking a much needed rest and viewing the world from your bedside.

XXXRodyXXX

Frontenac Arms
Toronto Nov. 24. 1945

QUEEN'S UNIVERSITY ARCHIVES: COLL. 2303.37, BOX 6, FILE 15, 1933-1964

Dear Isabel:

Herewith, your XXieme magazine – thanks for letting me have it, it is a beautiful book – I think I read every word and enjoyed it – I tried not to lose the marked places, in which you had put slips of paper.

AYJ phoned me this morning, re going to the Gallery at 2.30 p.m. tomorrow, for the 4th year Univ. students. I said I would be there – I phoned Miss Leonard at the Gallery to check and at first she said no it would be occupied by the York Memorial group, but then she said she had made a mistake the York Mem. was at 3.30 – so it is alright.

Toronto December 10th´1945   XXXRODYXXX

Also enclosed copy of M. Scott's letter re her canvases

QUEEN'S UNIVERSITY ARCHIVES: COLL. 2303.37, BOX 6, FILE 15, 1933-1964

Dear Isabel:

We are all missing you.

There was a luncheon today for the ballet people in town this week. It was small but very successful. Three different people said "Where is Miss McLaughlin – I haven't seen her lately.". Heliconian Club.

At a Promotion Committee meeting of the C.A.C., Paul Duval the chairman said "Maybe we could get Miss McLaughlin to help us – where is she?"

So you see they are missing you.

Jack Bush won the Rolph-Clark-Stone $500.00 prize at the OSA – I wasn't at the opening myself, but in spite of a very rainy night there was a good crowd they say. I like Bush's canvas – it is a "painters" [sic] canvas.

...I hear Panton is to be the Vice-Principal of the OCA – that's a good thing because in spite of a certain person saying he kills everything he touches I think he is a changed man and is ready to investigate new paths and I think he will be good for the school.

We had a CGP meeting at Paraskeva's last Thursday and I do wish there could be fuller meetings – is there not something in the constitution about quorums? Everything that had to be moved it was moved by Cass and seconded by me or vice versa. And most of the conversation was by – guess whom. (puss, puss).

Paul and I went to the Arts & Letters on Saturday night to see "Oblomoff" which the program described as "Portrait of a Russian gentleman – a play in 3 acts by John Coulter from the novel by Ivan Gontcharoff" – I liked it very much – it has been sold to a producer in NY.

Eric Aldwinkle was much praised and I thought Dicky Wagner was splendid.

Charles Comfort spoke at a luncheon at the Heliconian Club – I was sorry to miss it but I had a long standing date with some school teachers.

I have never told you about my trip to NY. There really isn't much to tell of interest about any of my trips there because I just visit galleries, schools etc. I was disappointed in the show at the Museum of Modern Art – it was a exhibition "Arts of the South Seas", all masks, spears, [?] and bamboo things which I somehow felt was not the business of the M of MA. I was just about to write them a letter telling them how much more important I felt it was for them to show modern painting, when I discovered in the current "New Yorker" that Robt. M. Coates had done just what I wanted to do.

The Whitney had a splendid scul[p]ture show, watercolors and drawings. The sculpture was in many mediums, or media if you are pedantic.

Norah was on the "Cavalcade" program just now and she came over splendidly, with noise effects & everything, telling about her three danger spots, while in Africa – five wild elephants; crocodiles they mistook for logs, and the wild natives. Her voice was very natural on the air.

…Love from the Courtices

Frontenac Arms,
Toronto. March 11´1946

QUEEN'S UNIVERSITY ARCHIVES: COLL. 2303.37, BOX 6, FILE 19, 1944-1966

En route (big trip) Toronto to Peterborough

Dear Isabel

I am on my way down to Peterborough to talk to the Peterborough Group of Painters and I thought it was a good opportunity to give you a report on the little happenings with us stay-at-homes.

First of all, the "Night of Crime" was a great success – $326.00 was the last report. Your canvas was very popular, many extra tickets being purchased for it. There were four works held over and above for special tickets – yours, won by an Anna Russell, advertised as "Canada's leading Commedienne" (Charles Goldhamer's fianceé) and playing at Eaton Auditorium soon; Dorothy Austin's won by Estelle Kew; and Estelle Kew's won by my maida, and mine won by a Mrs. Hastie. I was not at the club till 10:15 as I was speaking with a group at the gallery and on the way over to the Hel. Club I thought it would be fun to burst in and announce the house was pinched, but when I saw the crowd I refrained as it was so jammed I'm sure there would have been a panic trying to get out the fire door – In the afternoon of the Bingo D. Austin had said to me "Don't go around saying 'Are you coming to the Bingo at the Hel. Club tonight because we are just a little afraid of being pinched". I love Dorothy shushing anybody.

The night at the gallery for the Art Association was not as well attended as they had hoped – 110 people – when Charlie Band asked where all the C.G.P. members were, both Peter and I said we had had no notice – and Charlie said "A.Y. was at the meeting and [was] supposed to notify all the C.G.P.," so you see Isabel when we haven't got you, there is a let-down.

Love,
Rody

POST MARK MARCH 14, 1946
QUEEN'S UNIVERSITY ARCHIVES: COLL. 2303.37, BOX 6, FILE 19, 1944-1966

Dear Izzy:

In Branford [sic] working with seventy-odd (?) school teachers.

A most beautiful June-April morning – the natives said it was 1¾ miles to the Bell Homestead – when I walked there the plaque in the museum said it was 3 miles – so I've done six miles before 12 noon.

Isn't it time you were coming home!

Best to the clan McLaughlin –
Brantford   xxRodyxx

April 2/46

QUEEN'S UNIVERSITY ARCHIVES: COLL. 2303.37, BOX 6, FILE 19, 1944-1966

Dear Isabel:

Sorry I could not speak to you on the phone last night but I knew it was useless as the previous night I got into a bad fix not being able to hear and everybody else in bed and I just had to explain and ring off. I'll have to see an ear doctor first thing when we get in next week. We expect to be at the Frontenac on the 15th or 16th Oct. Wa. 3390.

I regret I cannot accept your nice invitation to coctails [sic] before the dinner at the Hel Club on the 9th but I know I must stay put for a little while. Lorna must be bursting with excitement having a Director at Hart House, but I am also afraid I cannot manage even that luncheon on [the] 16th.

On the Saturday on which you called, at 9.p.m. Paul's temperature finally hit 104.2 and I was practically beside him all night. In the morning the doctor from Agincourt pronounced it pneumonia and put him on sulpha every four hours. I looked after him myself and getting up at 3 a.m. to change his bed and give sulpha is what has retarded me. He is on the mend again and I hope we are now on the healthy list again.

I realize that the four-women show in January and a Group show in April is a pretty big order, but it seems to me it is just what we should be doing – painting more and more and I think it would liven things up in the Group. Should the membership be canvassed first to see if it will be popular? Do you not think that some canvases from previous shows could be included as many of the public would never have seen them in the Gallery. And of course painting all new canvases and showing them at Eatons precludes using them in any other Gallery exhibitions.

I know there should be a meeting of the Group Executive and also of the four-women group and I would be available (God willing) after Oct. 16th, except

Oct. 21st in the evening. If there must be a meeting before the 16th, you will just have to count me out. I, for one, appreciate your playing Guardian Angel over the group, Isabel, in the absence of the Pres. and I think by some it is taken for granted that you are the one holding the interest of the group together.

Love, Rody

R.R. 1, Markham,
Oct. 8th´1946

QUEEN'S UNIVERSITY ARCHIVES: COLL. 2303.37, BOX 6, FILE 17, 1939-1969

Dear Isabel:

You are the belle of the four damsels in the picture which appeared in last Saturday's Globe-Mail and you and Yvonne were wise in wearing something white against your faces – it would have been a good thing if I had thought to do the same. It really was quite a spread and very nice of Pearl McCarthy to give us so much space.

I have been wondering if before everybody gets away for the holidays, a few would care to come to the country for lunch with me – you and Gladys, Yvonne, Evelyn, Betty,. Would you? Even without any help I think I could keep you from being hungry.

You still have me stymied about the picture of mine which you said you had bought – each time I have seen you I have forgotten to find out from you. In any case, I would be more than pleased if it could be made an exchange, if you have one of yours you would part with.

We have a God given pool this year, water over my head in one spot, and you can swim 25 or 30 strokes.

I will phone you about the time I think you have this and if you can come I will phone the others.

Any red marks on this letter are wild strawberry kisses, as I have just finished picking two pints,…

Rody

R.R. 1, Markham
July 7´1947

QUEEN'S UNIVERSITY ARCHIVES: COLL. 2303.37, BOX 6, FILE 15, 1933-1964

DEAR
ISABEL!
  WELL!
IT. IS.A.SWELL!
  SMELL!

and thank you very much.

We wish you a happy, happy New Year.

At this time I would like to say a big thanks from Roy and me for the dinner parties, the Royal Winter Fair one and the C.G.P. Executive one. We enjoyed them.

Also I would like to say you and Yvonne were greatly missed at the C.G.P. Annual meetings.

Best, Rody

F.A.

Jan. 8/48

QUEEN'S UNIVERSITY ARCHIVES: COLL. 2303.37, BOX 6, FILE 17, 1939-1969

Dear Isabel

When I realized the beautiful block print was conveying a subscription for "Here and Now" you can imagine how thrilled I was – I have only seen a copy (already sold) at Dahers, for a few minutes, but I was impressed with the undertaking and very curious – I recall getting a circular about it. There does not seem to be a signature to the block print but I presume it is Laurence Hyde. We thank you very much and are looking forward to the arrival of the first number.

...As you were one of the hanging committee for the C.G.P. I am wondering who went instead of you. I hear Charles Comfort did not send any – I saw a non-objective one of his in Keith's ready for a western show, which I thought most interesting.

Roy and I are off to see "Hamlet" about which I have heard such conflicting reports.

We wish you and Co.. and Mrs. McLaughlin happiness for the New Year and with love from the three Courtices.

Rody

3027 Queen E.
Toronto Dec 29 – 1948.

QUEEN'S UNIVERSITY ARCHIVES: COLL. 2303.37, BOX 6, FILE 17, 1939-1969

RODY KENNY COURTICE

COPY

Isabel

Dear Bobs, Isabel and Yvonne:
The below is a note which I have sent to Mrs McQuillan and is self-explanatory.
Best regards,
Sincerely, Rody

Mrs. McQuillan,
"Chatelaine"
401 University Ave,
Toronto, Ont.

Dear Mrs. McQuillan,
I apologize for bothering you about your article on the "Four-Women" but there is one small item which I would like to have corrected.

It is always my contention when speaking to groups or persons concerning art education, that while experience in any school can be helpful, it is not essential to have attended schools abroad. I therefore, wondered if the paragraph commencing something like this "All have studied in Europe" … might contain the following information concerning me:

Mrs. Courtice was not registered in any school but painted and sketched with other students in London, Paris, Venice and Milan, etc., attending croquis classes in several schools.

If you refer to the printed sheet I gave you, you will note that I mentioned only croquis classes and sketching.

I am afraid you will think this is splitting hairs, but as recently as last December, in speaking to one hundred dentists and their wives at the Art Gallery of Toronto, I was in quite an argument with them on this very point and I would hate to have that many dentists writing me and saying "What about this?"

I enjoyed your report on the four of us and realized you had all you ears working in the hubbub that went on at Mrs. Haworth's that day.

With kind regards,
Yours sincerely
Rody Kenny Courtice

R.R. 1,
Markham, Ont,
May 7' 1948

Dear Isabel

How nice of you to write me so soon from Bermuda – things move so fast – I had hardly realized you had gone.

...I have heard good reports from many Heliconians on the party – and I went in last Thursday to have a look – you really must take care of your decoration – it is terrifically strong I think.

Getting back to the Hel party you didn't tell me if you wore a costume – perhaps it is just as well that I had a temperature and couldn't go because this is probably the way I would have looked:

[drawing by artist]

as I had only a black hat with an ostrich black feather Ronny McRae had loaned me – black gloves and black high boots.

I realize the buttons are on the wrong side of the boots but I take artistic privilege.

...Thank you very much for the lovely "Picasso" gray and white place mats – most acceptable – I do not comprehend how you get it all done – I came home after going for a short walk on Friday and the parcel was at the door and I thought I had missed you but I realize it must have been someone else who left it. Thanks again.

...Your card is most attractive and it caused a lot of pleasing comments.

...With love and thanks
Rody

39 Whitehall
Dec 27/49

QUEEN'S UNIVERSITY ARCHIVES: COLL. 2303.37, BOX 6, FILE 17, 1939-1969

Dear Isabel

Greetings!! To yourself, to Co. and Mrs McLaughlin, to Mary Owen, to Betty and to all other lucky <u>northerners</u> southing down there.

Thank you ever so much for the lovely, lovely luncheon set, Canadien – I felt like <u>wearing</u> it someway so that more people would see it.

And we loved the Bermuda Bouganvillea – Paul was particularly interested because he is studying Botany. (Paul was in Collingwood for New Years skiing and saw Bobs and Peter).

Tell Mary congratulations from Roy because he heard she had sold some of her lovely photographs to Southern Press – getting commercial just like the rest of us, I say. Also thanks to Col. And Mrs McLaughlin for the most attractive Xmas card and again congrats. to Mary for the "Trillium <u>scene</u>".

I had a card from Polly Parker and Mrs Jackson, both a la Hofmann – I suppose you did also.

Everywhere people are asking for you, when are you returning, etc., etc.

Love and best wishes for the year,
Rody

290 St. Clair E.
Toronto Jan 12/50.

QUEEN'S UNIVERSITY ARCHIVES: COLL. 2303.37, BOX 6, FILE 20, 1951-1961

Dear Isabel

Greetings!

It seems another lifetime since our sojourn to the Cape. The contrast between Provincetown and Haliburton is interesting – the flora and the fauna particularly. The fauna up here has suffered some with the tent caterpillar scourge this year.

It was a most successful trip in my estimation, the Cape one I mean, made attractive by having your Hydrmatic [sic] and being associated with two such wonderful "femmes de voyage". Think of the porridge we ate and all the dishes you washed. I am still chewing on "push and pull" and "too much ver-ticality" etc., etc. I miss stepping off each morning to the studio. Thank you for including me in the trip.

…Love from Rody

Gull Lake
July 28/50.

QUEEN'S UNIVERSITY ARCHIVES: COLL. 2303.37, BOX 6, FILE 15, 1933-1964

Dear Isabel:

It was a wonderful dinner party Friday at the Ladies' Club before the C.G.P. show. I hope you were not too exhausted after the whole affair because I know how tired you were getting, the day before.

Your "Nugget Dance Hall" is most amusing, but more than that – it is a beautifully executed piece of painting.

Love Rody

290 St. Clair E.
Nov 17/50

QUEEN'S UNIVERSITY ARCHIVES: COLL. 2303.37, BOX 6, FILE 15, 1933-1964

Dear Isabel:

To give you a report right away on the exhibition to hang in the Heliconian Club for February – it is to be Gordon MacNamara's, coming from the Picture Loan Soc.

I tried to find out where the Leonard Brook's ex. was, but nobody seemed to know. Dick Van has about eight unframed water colors which he said he might arrange to let us have, but I took a look at them and decided they were not colorful enough and too few of them. In the meantime before I received your letter A.Y.J. had phoned me that you had approached him about an ex. for the Hel. club for Feb. and suggested Phyllis Hipwell Janes (a cousin of Dr. Fred Bantings's) – she had just had a show at the Picture Loan – I agreed that I thought it would be alright although I did not see her show and from what I remembered of her work when we were at school together, it struck me as "lagylike" [ladylike?]. However, it was not available because it had been distributed and could not be collected again, or something like that. A.Y.J suggested that we ask Kay Pepper, which I did but after considering it for one night she called me up and said as she is facing an operation on her back (an old wound flaring up) she felt she couldn't get a show ready. Then I tried Rene Cera – who also considered it for a night and refused regretfully. Next was Estelle Kerr, who considered it for four hours (I told her I couldn't give her longer) and said she felt she hadn't enough and couldn't amass enough frames. She suggested Murray Bonneycastle, whom I did not call. But this morning I called Gord. Mac. and he accepted with pleasure and am I relieved. Now in all these cases, (except Rene Cera) I used your name as having suggested them so if you are thanked by each of them when you return, for having asked them, you will understand. Gordon's show will not be available till Feb. 5th, but Miss Sharpe said that would be alright – we would keep the Xmas decor. up till then. This will go in the bulletin for Feb. together with a notation for the members of art sec. to be prepared with three or four works for Mar. ex, card later.

Vida asked me to tell you that she has a ticket for you for the Opera Festival for Feb. 8th.

Sat. night is Hel-Arts & Letters night – wish you three were here. However, any of us would take the Barbadoes instead.

...As usual in a rush!!!!!!

Rody

290 St. Clair E
Toronto, Thursday, Jan 25′1951

QUEEN'S UNIVERSITY ARCHIVES: COLL. 2303.37, BOX 6, FILE 15, 1933-1964

Dear Isabel:

Saw Marg McLaughlin yesterday – she came up for tea and we discussed arrangements for a sketching trip. She said she had been speaking to you and that you were feeling a little better and expected to be in Oshawa on Sunday and thought you might make our "do". Seeing that you are one of the "raison d'etres" we shall be very disappointed if we do not have you. Everybody seems to be coming, those we were able to ask.

About the trip, as I said before the only way I could be comfortable until I get my show hung is to stay at home. But also I would not be comfortable if you and Y. changed any plans. I feel that you should go where and when it suits you and I will try and follow up if you are still away when I am free.

Hope to see you Sunday,
Love Rody

Wed, Sept. 26′51

QUEEN'S UNIVERSITY ARCHIVES: COLL. 2303.37, BOX 6, FILE 18, 1941-1953

Dear Marg [Alexandra Luke]

Congratulations for a most stimulating exhibition – I think it is very thought-giving and am counting on having another look at it.

And Roy and I very much appreciated being included in your dinner party.

Mary is a most attractive girl and I liked meeting her and her husband – a very eye-catching pair.

Love
Rody

290 St. Clair E
Toronto Mar. 23/52
THE ROBERT MCLAUGHLIN GALLERY ARCHIVES: BOX 2, FILE 1

Dear Isabel

This is to put on written record my appreciation of your including me in the Laurentian painting trip – I enjoyed it immensely and want to thank you at this time for the many thoughtful things you do.

…This is also my thanks as a member of the C.G.P. for the enormous undertaking of having such a large group after the show at your apartment – such delightful refreshments, of which, alas, I was unable to have any.

(Roy is either writing or phoning you his apologies for the argument he and Aba got into – and in this connection I wanted to say I do not think the drinks figured as I believe Aba had had none and I am sure Roy had only gingerale, as I had) Love, Rody

Sunday Nov 2/52
QUEEN'S UNIVERSITY ARCHIVES: COLL. 2303.37, BOX 6, FILE 19, 1944-1966

Dear Isabel

This small basket of breakfast jam was scheduled to be at your apartment to greet you when you arrived home – but you fooled me by coming home sooner than expected – I just finished "hand painting" the labels and as I did them with that good "BLOOKX" water color which we got in Provincetown (I am sure it is mixed with egg white or something slow drying) the paint is slow drying and is probably all stuck to the wrapper.

This jam is meant for your Sylvan retreat but you don't have to prove to me you ate it.

Love from Rody

290 St. Clair E.
Wed. Jan 28/53

PS. I notice the plastic glue I used on the labels has an odor but I assure you it did not get near the contents.

QUEEN'S UNIVERSITY ARCHIVES: COLL. 2303.37, BOX 6, FILE 20, 1951-1961

Dear Isabel

Greetings!

Herewith cheque for $2.44 for gas re Laurentians – I had not forgotten and hoped to hand it to you on first opportunity – I still maintain the "conductor" of the tour should not have been troubled with either the expense or the accounting of the gas.

I hope your recovery is progressing – I phoned you twice last week to see how you were – and to seek advice about writing to Randolph – I just don't seem to be able to do it – the subject is so overwhelming. Also I wanted assistance on how to tell a woman here from Paris (her husband attached to an estate business in France with the Tor. Gen Trust) what the Hel. Club is, when I took her there at her request to see it. "Professional women in the arts" translated into my French might have turned us all into street walkers. Love, Rody

290 St. Clair E.
Wed. Jan 29/53

QUEEN'S UNIVERSITY ARCHIVES: COLL. 2303.37, BOX 6, FILE 19, 1944-1966

Dear Isabel:

I have been going to drop you a note for sometime. I have been thinking about you but seem to have been so snowed under with interruptions and annoyances that I am too tired at the end of the day to do anything but go to bed.

As you know we bought a house, 60 Glenhowan Rd. We started right in to make some changes and I do not know whether it was the length of time it took to do what I thought was quite a small job, or what, but I have realized that I do not want a city house – it is too much responsibility, as long as we have the country – I'll be doing nothing but run from one to the other looking after maintenance jobs. I have thought all along that I wanted a house in the city so we could eliminate all this moving we have been doing and because what we could afford to rent was so inadequate, but I feel now I'd rather be back in an apartment. It is a well built house and small but needs so many changes to make it our kind of a house that I just feel I can't face it. I think Roy feels it will have to be put up for sale and of course, if sold, that means looking for and furnishing another apartment. That alone, makes me exhausted, just to think of it.

I saw Yvonne and we had a lovely evening last Wednesday at which we had hoped to see you.

I wanted you and Gladys and Yvonne to know I'm in one of those states when I am ready to cry over quite small annoyances and I recognize I need checking up and rest. But I am thinking about you, and hope to bounce back one of these days. Please do not think I am looking for sympathy, but just wanted you to know why I am a missing number.

Love from
Rody

R.R. 1,
Markham, Ont
June 29th '1953

QUEEN'S UNIVERSITY ARCHIVES: COLL. 2303.37, BOX 6, FILE 18, 1941-1953

Dear Isabel

Greetings!

At the meeting of our committee (Paraskeva and I) with the C.G.P. Ex last night we were alotted [sic] names to notify on certain points and you are on my list.

FIRST IT IS TO BE IMPRESSED on us that we must be at the Studio Bldg the night of the 22nd at or before 10:30, before Mr. Massey arrives. SECOND a list of all names of guests must be submitted prior to Oct 22nd. In this connection if you have a name, Chas. Comfort who has this in charge, has asked that the name be phoned to Louis Comfort.

These points are in accord with instructions from aid-de-camp of the G.G.

After listening to the strict procedure and solemnity of the occasion Para and I mutually agreed that a "nood lady" would be in bad taste and shock A.Y. (To say nothing of the others). A.Y. seems to be very impressed with the importance of the event and I feel we should do nothing to minimize it.

There is only a small (about 3') table in Alex studio but Para thinks that a card table of hers and one you said you had would do – added to the above. I feel crepe paper would also be wrong – Para said she had some white cloths. She will probably phone you about it. I feel a little anxious about it as this is no Bohemian affair but very cut-and-dried performance I think.

Love Rody

Oct 15/53

QUEEN'S UNIVERSITY ARCHIVES: COLL 2303.37, BOX 6, FILE 21, 1953-1955

Cheers!! For Alexandra Luke – only woman showing in Simpsons Abstract – clever idea and yours look wonderful in, of all things, "French Provincial".

Rody

POST CARD TO MRS. EWART MCLAUGHLIN (ALEXANDRA LUKE), POST MARK OCTOBER 28, 1953
THE ROBERT MCLAUGHLIN GALLERY ARCHIVES: BOX 2, FILE 1

Dear Isabel:

Greetings!!

At the symphony last night 'twas said you were home working, which I felt I should have been doing but I was in such a bad mess on my largest canvas, it was hopeless.

The sad news that greeted us when we arrived home from our Eastern "toor" was that Hurricane Hazel had blown down about seventeen of our trees, mostly by the roots and the "Isabel McLaughlin" Weeping Willow at the N.E. corner of the house is no more.

In the face of what happened [to] the people on the Humber, we cannot groan too loudly, but we could hardly believe it could have happened. The farmer said the ten days previous heavy rains softened the ground so much, the roots had no purchase against the 90-mile wind.

But we loved her while we had her –
"THE ISABEL MCLAUGHLIN
WEEPING WILLOW".

Love from
Rody

30 Elm Ave
Toronto Oct. 27′54

QUEEN'S UNIVERSITY ARCHIVES: COLL. 2303.37, BOX 6, FILE 17, 1939-1969

Dear Isabel

Your yellow chrysanthemums which you sent us have been a great delight – very lovely – bunches of sunshine in our north light. Thanks very much.

And thanks also for the very enjoyable driver (O.S.A.) And being "Caddilac-ed" to and from the gallery. Very easy to take.

Love Rody

30 Elm Ave.
Jan 10/55

QUEEN'S UNIVERSITY ARCHIVES: COLL 2303.37, BOX 6, FILE 21, 1953-1955

Dear Isabel:

I had the pleasure of taking Gladys Montgomery, Dr. Ann Curtin and AYJ down to Oshawa last Thursday to view your mural in the Oshawa Library. It is a very lovely piece of work and we were all very proud of you as we sat in front of it. The Oshawa people are very lucky to have this mural in "your" beautiful library.

Love from Rody

30 elm ave
toronto, feb. 1´55

Dear Alex:

I've had 'flu for four days and am only now getting back to wiggling again. I expect others to have 'flu but not myself.

It is a queer feeling to not be able to phone you and realize that you are not over in the studio building, but I do think yours was a great move and you will be more and more in love with your "castle" as time goes on. It sounds wonderful – the kitchen, and a bedroom that gets the first peep of the sun.

You certainly started off with a burst by addressing the Women's Can. Club – I knew they would be trailing you – you will be bombarded from every side.

At the O.C.A. students exhibition I had tea with Eugenia Berlin who had as a guest (here for O.E.A.) a Mrs. Beament, whose husband is a lawyer in Ottawa. She was telling me that their home is just beside the place where you are going to be for a summer school.

As you know the Comforts were due to get out of their apartment by May 1st. They approached us about renting our apartment and we would have been glad to have them but Roy has too many meetings in town for us to leave before the 15th of May at earliest and we probably won't go out till June, as I do not want to run the furnace which is coal fed. Rumor says the Comforts are to have your studio, so that would put Charles back in the studio he once had.

I haven't been able to interest anyone in "Verve" The Painter, The Model and Picasso – but I know Mary Jackman gets "Verve" and if I get a look at it I'll let you know.

Last week the jury sat on the C.S.P.W.C. (I was a member) – a great amount submitted – show being opened this Friday by A. Lismer.

I got such a pleasant surprise seeing your "Au Revoir" show – I did not know it was going up. It made a great attraction for the gallery goers, in the

East square gallery.

...On Friday, May 13th, Curator Jarvis of the Nat. Gal. is coming up to present the awards at the O.C.A.

On every hand people are asking about you and I'm sure you are going to need a social secretary to look after your correspondence.

The big T.S.O. auction sale is on today and tomorrow and I am off to help police the Thieves Market (Dorothy Austin's booth), at Varsity Stadium – the light fingered just swarm in there. They made Fifteen Thousand last year and hope to beat that this year. "Never underestimate the Power of Woman".

I've seen Yvonne, looks wonderful, and had dinner with Isabel, Chet and Betty Harris (Betty Kimbark) and when I asked them if Lawren painted while in Arizona they said "Yes, but we never saw any of it". Chet is Lawren's first cousin.

Love from us, always and glad to get your note.
Rody

Rosedale Court, Apt. 204
30 Elm Ave
Toronto, May 3/55

NATIONAL ARCHIVES CANADA, MG: M630D351; FILE 26; VOLUME 82

Isabel McLaughlin

HELICONIAN CLUB

The convenors of the Art Section of the Heliconian Club wish to thank all those members who so generously contributed to the exhibition and sale of works at the "Meadow Lark" at Polly Harris' "Sheepfold" on June 21/56. Below is reference to your particular work:

1 work sold to Mrs. Henderson
1 work " " Yvonne Housser

All work unsold, unless collected at the "Meadow Lark", is at the Heliconian Club and should be collected on or before June 28th/56 between the hours: 10 to 12 a.m. and 2. to 4.pm, otherwise it will remain in the club till fall.

Convenors:
Isabel McLaughlin
Rody Kenny Courtice

Dear Isabel: Greetings!!

I took the liberty of writing this over your name as co-convenor, as it had to go out quickly, in order that unsold works to be picked up, if wanted, before Miss Sharpre leaves on her vacation on June 28th./ Hope you approve. A copy went to every member who had contributed.

Love, Rody

POST MARK JUNE 25, 1958
QUEEN'S UNIVERSITY ARCHIVES: COLL. 2303.37, BOX 6, FILE 20, 1951-1961

Dear Alex:

Greetings!!

Nice to have a letter from you.

I have not finished reading your "Painter's Country", savoring every word. It will be interesting reading for anybody but for me it is fascinating, and of course, fills me with nostalgia. I started at the Ontario College of Art in the fall term of 1920, when it was still in the old Model School. I soon became acquainted with all your names and was very aware of what was going on, through listening to Mr. Lismer when he would come back from the Arts & Letters Club after having had lunch listening to Hector Charlesworth, etc. And later, in the second year when I was put on the staff I was privileged to gather at breaks, in the corner studio, when we got a lot of backwash of what the Group was doing. It was a thrilling time for you Seven – it was even thrilling for us just to be in the atmosphere of what you were doing. And so, in reading your book, I can reflect back on the very time a particular event happened. Because of your humorous handling it is an easy book to read and it is wonderful to have gotten all this information between two covers. I ordered my copy at the reception of Clarke-Irwin building but only picked it up after I came home from Florida. There is a good display of the deluxe edition in the cases at the Gallery.

Isabel and I went to a lecture last Wed. night at the art gallery, Dr. Alfred M Frankfurter on "Tintoretto and Modernity", very dull – the points he tried to make I found quite unconvincing and I.G. said she felt the same way – a sales talk for the Tintoretto. I don't mind telling you that I find the Tintoretto dull too – I was telling Marg. Machell I think it is a fake and she said they had had a letter from a woman who says she knows and can prove it is a fake, of course these rumors always get around and what difference does it make as far as the public is concerned – they will still stand around in awe at those romantic figures with beards. But I do think the incident in connection with TV publicity was amusing. Perhaps you heard that they wanted a dog of the breed shown in the foreground of the canvas and finally found Dr. Williams (veterinarian) had one and asked her to bring it at a certain time to the Gallery. When she arrived the guards would not let her in until they got the curator – very gentle dog – tried to lick everyone's ears.

...When Paul was here at the beginning of Feb. he took two of his books from the "Jackson Library"–: "Wai, Wai" and "the Rideau Waterway" to Kemptville – I hope he takes care of them and brings them back.

The Lady of the Snow is certainly being a slut the way the snow is being thrown around. Roy and I went out to the country yesterday and spent the afternoon shovelling snow drifts away from doors and hacking at ice to try to keep the drains open because it looks as if we are in for flooded cellars this year. And then this morning a very heavy snow fall, starting at seven o'clock a.m.

...Referring again to "A Painter's Country" you can imagine how complimented Roy and I are to be "among those present". Also, when you mention Norah [McCullough] going to Africa as Mr. Lismer's assistant, you know Mr. Lismer offered that job to me first. It was a difficult decision to make but I turned it down and recommended Norah – I often wonder where I would have ended up if I had accepted. Norah was excellently suited for it and has made a notable contribution and never retreated when she disagreed with A.L. I was with Mr. Lismer on the children's classes from 1927 till they closed – I'm sure Norah could write a book herself about that period. (I have never felt that A.L. gave Norah, or Audrey, or in fact any of us, credit (in his "September Gale") for the loyal support we gave him during that time at the Gallery – certainly we got no adequate financial reward. I sound catty!!!!!![)]

Helen Band was telling me that Mrs. Lismer had been in hospital, was home, better, but feeling dispirited so I wrote her a little note – hope she now is more robust – she is such a solace for A.L. – what would he do without her.

As the snow still falls I'll get lost again in "A Painter's Country". If I haven't already wished you a good year I hope you continue to have a rousing success in the balance of 1959.

Best from us all,
Rody

Rosedale Court – Apt. 204
30 elm ave.
toronto – 5, February 23/1959

NATIONAL ARCHIVES CANADA, MG: M630D351; FILE 24, VOLUME 91

Dear Isabel

Thank you for a most enjoyable Ottawa trip – a most delightful way to travel – beautiful companions, beautiful car – beautifully driven – beautiful weather.

And I have already used the lovely coddler you gave me – it's a lovely idea especially for a tray.

So glad you included me in the National Gallery Tour –

Love, Rody

Rosedale Court
Toronto – 5 – July 4/60

P.S. Received from Art Section Hel. notice – it is "in my mirror" Efficient and Timely you!!!

QUEEN'S UNIVERSITY ARCHIVES: COLL. 2303.37, BOX 6, FILE 20, 1951-1961

from: r.k. courtice   Copies sent to: Mrs. Pratt
                                               Mrs. Murray
                                               Miss McLaughlin
                                               Mrs. Craig.

Report to the Convenors of Book Plate and Christmas card.
Heliconian Club

Book Plate

Before the sad loss of Miss Edith Macdonald I saw her three times when we were intending to use the fireplace design. When the present design was ready and I phoned her she said she was too uncomfortable to see anybody.

I saw Mrs. Pratt and she passed it, with a reservation about the small printing, which could not be changed without making a new plate.

I phoned Mrs Murray but expect she was still out of town.

300 Book Plates to be printed.

Christmas Card

Miss McLaughlin came several times to the printer with me and saw him again at my apartment and gave some valuable criticism. I took the off-set proofs up to Miss McLaughlin.

Mrs. Craig made the initial trip to the printer with me – her suggestion was that a large card as well as a small one be ordered, which I think was valuable. Mrs. Craig was not in town at the time the off-set proofs came through.

1000 small Christmas Cards to be printed
1000 large   "   "   "

The printer expects to have all the above ready in about two weeks.

May I suggest that the convenors of the Christmas Card arrange to have a selling notice inserted in the first Hel. bulletin. I am dropping a note to Miss Blake asking her to check with the convenors.

Rody

Rosedale Court
Toronto August 30th/1960

QUEEN'S UNIVERSITY ARCHIVES: COLL. 2303.37, BOX 6, FILE 20, 1951-1961

Dear Isabel:

Greetings!!
    Attached is a report on the water color show you saw in the Brooklyn Museum – just in case you did not see it in the May 13/61 "New Yorker" – rather interesting reading some one else's crit after you have assessed it for yourself. Wish I had seen this show, it closes May 28th. If the Jaenisch "Fisherman's Dream" was a negro boy with an oversize fish in a boat it is a very old picture.

Thought this might be of interest to you,
Love Rody

Wed. May 17/1961

QUEEN'S UNIVERSITY ARCHIVES: COLL. 2303.37, BOX 6, FILE 20, 1951-1961

"The Moorings"
127 S E 7th Ave
Delray Beach – FLA
Jan 7 – 62

Dear Isabel

Greetings!

   …I see by the G + M the Royal Academy opens next Friday and the big
excitement about the $2000 winner will be announced. I hear the jury shovelled
[sic] many out (mine among them). Did you send?

QUEEN'S UNIVERSITY ARCHIVES: COLL. 2303.37, BOX 6, FILE 17, 1939-1969

Dear Isabel

Greetings!!

   What a lovely gift I received from you at Christmas time – the lovely long
gloves. My wrists should no longer be cold – with the shorter coat sleeves these
gloves are ideal – I have been wearing my ski mitts because they covered my
wrists. Thanks for your thoughtfulness.

   …We left Toronto Dec 29th in very reasonable weather but at Buffalo
ran into a blizzard.

   …Although I brought water colours and crayons, I have spent most of
my time walking on the beach – "me" and the gulls, as very few walk, which
suits me.

   We have this apartment to the end of January, after which we may stay
for a little longer or go over to the west coast.

Roy and I send love and best wishes for the coming year.
Rody

Tuesday Jan 9/62

QUEEN'S UNIVERSITY ARCHIVES: COLL. 2303.37, BOX 6, FILE 17, 1939-1969

Dear Alex:

Greetings!!

Everyone seems to know that "A.Y.J." is going to the Yukon and now the papers are announcing it. I would think the Flag Committee would be on your heels and interfering with your trip.

We did some running around, Peterborough, Port Hope, etc, and went to Lake Simcoe but the weather was so bad we came home – August was a lost month, the worst, I think.

Isabel called me one day to say Bess Harris was in town on one of her flying trips and could I have lunch with them and Audrey Taylor, so the four of us had a lovely talking about you all, and the pros and cons of the "SEVEN" – I think it is six years since I saw Bess and she just looks the same. She said Lawren Jr. was in Vancouver staying with Lawren Sr. while she was here.

…A Mr. Lawrence Nowry phoned me some weeks ago, said he was from the CBC, wanted to do a tape on the "Group of Seven". He made an appointment, then broke it, and by then I was going out. But later I got a note from him from Ottawa making another date which he kept and I presume he is the one you mention in your letter, – he said he was most pleased with the time and material you gave him. I always wish after one of this kind of thing has taken place that I had said altogether different things. I think a questionnaire submitted before hand would help – we are not all as easy in speaking as you are!!!

I am having my usual bout with hay fever.

We have a good looking invitation from the Dresdnere Gallery and are looking forward to Thurs. Sept. 17th and to seeing you.

Best from us
Rody

Rosedale Court – 204, 30 elm ave, tor – 5, Sept. 12/1964

P.S. – I hear F. Horseman Varley has a Lincoln!!!

NATIONAL ARCHIVES CANADA, MG: M630D351; FILE 8; VOLUME 92

RODY KENNY COURTICE

Dear Alex:

Greetings greetings greetings!!!!

This is to say that we have been following the traveller Doctor Alexander Young Jackson by reading the newspapers, by reading all the newspapers he is in the yukon his picture is in the papers he is in lake superior his picture is in the newspapers that is to say all the newspapers working working working meeting fog and snow but ayj that is to say doctor alexander young jackson is working working working.

You will gather that I have been reading Gertrude Stein and am affected by it. Which I have been doing. Did you ever meet her, wish I had. We have here in the apartment the lovely Stein book you gave Paul Courtice in 1939 (when he was eight years old) "The World is Round" printed on rosey rosey rosey paper!

We have mostly stayed in the city this summer, going out on jaunts to Port Hope, Peterborough, Lake Simcoe and Bobcaygeon, Haliburton, etc.

Mary Jackman had a very pleasant gathering at her house on the Sunday that the Group of Seven was broadcast. It was quite good but I think it could have been better, not enough showing of the Seven. Wonder if you saw it.

We saw you in the broadcast of the Loring-Wyle – wonderful to have this record of the "Girls", with you and Keith, etc.

Audrey Taylor was here in June and we had dinner with her and Isabel and discussed old times.

Papers will be full of election news, I supposed, until it is over. Sometimes I think I will vote Conservative and then decide I'll vote Liberal – if only we knew how to get a party with a working majority – otherwise I do not think there is much choice.

As ever as ever as ever as ever
Rody

Rosedale Court – 204
30 elm ave, tor – 5
September 21/1965

NATIONAL ARCHIVES CANADA, MG: M630D351; FILE 26; VOLUME 82

Dear Alex:

Greetings!!

Imagine my disturbed surprise when I heard two days ago that you were or had been in hospital. The information I had was that you were having trouble with the inner ear. I know how distressing this can be because Roy has experienced it, twice, and it is most upsetting. I hope that it has all cleared by now and that you are back to normal.

I cannot write this letter without speaking of the sad, sad going of Keith McIver – it is hard to believe that the gentle Keith is gone – he seemed to be such a fixture that nothing could disturb. I only heard about this a few days ago, also.

As a matter of fact I have been in hospital myself for ten days – my doctor was quite sure that, like President Johnston, I was staging a gall bladder operation. However, having been X-rayed from tip to toe, all seems clear and I am relying on home treatment under doctor's orders. While I was in hospital (I discourage all callers and flowers when I am ill), for amusement, I did a small book of Gertrude Stein's "Conversation as Explanation" in shorthand, for practice. I did a page at a time, then checked it with a shorthand dictionary – what an occupation!! but it amused the nurses who finally got to know who Gertrude Stein was.

Thank you for sending my small sketch to Norah DePencier for Owen Sound – I am complimented.

About your birthday party at McMichaels (your birthday, like all Christian holy-days seems to be a movable feast), Yvonne said she telephoned us but did not reach us – to bad to miss your party but thanks for thinking of us.

With all good wished for health and happiness, from Roy and
Rody

Sunday, Dec. 19/1965

NATIONAL ARCHIVES CANADA, MG: M630D351; FILE 26; VOLUME 82

Dear Isabel:

Greetings!!!

…The two hot subjects in Toronto just now are the Subway and whether or not to tear down the Old City Hall. Strong feelings are displayed and I am glad to see such interest taken. Prof. J.H. Acland, School of Architecture, Un. Of Toronto, was the guest speaker on Wed. Feb. 23 at a Hel. luncheon. He belonged to the "Don't Tear Down" group and I felt there should have been a speaker for the "Tear Down" group. I had not planned to go but got a call from the secretary asking if she might put my name down. I recognized it as a cry for help and signed up. I was at a table of fifteen, members and guests. I was beside Margaret Aitken and we decided to canvas the table and found three "not to tear" and twelve for demolition. It is claimed that the architects as a group favor the preserving the o.c.h. but in an article in the press a week ago John Parkin said it was the voice of only 200 architects out of the some 1700 members and that implicit in the building of the new was the destruction of the old. My suggestion is that if so many wish to retain the o.c.h., let's tear down the new c.h., because they cannot live together!

It is very strange not having street cars any more on Bloor Street, where I walk so much. It does not seem possible to miss street cars passing but I do. Roy and I took a test trip on the Bloor-Danforth subway, leaving Sherbourne station we travelled west to Keele St., back east to University, down University to the Union Station, north to Bloor and back east to Sherbourne St., without changing trains. Do you recall that you and I opened the Yonge St. subway? I missed you this time.

Rosedale Court – 204
30 Elm Ave, Toronto – 5
March 4, 1966

QUEEN'S UNIVERSITY ARCHIVES: COLL. 2303.37, BOX 6, FILE 19, 1944-1966

Dear Alex:

Greetings!!

Glad to hear from you in your letter of June 17/66. You do get around and every time I hear of you, you are in a different place. Nice seeing Bess and Lawren. When Lawren Jr. was here some time ago (for the Group-of-Seven dinner at the Royal York) he told me that Lawren could only concentrate for about twenty minutes at a time. It must be a strain on Bess. I have been wondering if you saw Fran and Harry Adaskin and their unique house, with the two grand pianos in the living room.

Of course we read all about your receiving the LL.D from the University of B.C., and I have been wondering if I should now address your letters with 2-LL.D's!!!

I thought the article entitled "A.Y. Jackson-Portrait of an Artist", in the Telegram Weekend Magazine of April 30/66 was well done. Good pictures of you – I could smell the snow – only those who have painted in snow know what a special thrill it can be.

Mona Cannon saw you on television twice but we only saw you the once (with Florence, Frances and Keith) awfully good.

…We are going through the throes of having the walls of the apartment painted – everything piled in the middle of the floor – everything misplaced, probably for the next year.

…A week ago Saturday Mona's house was on display, one of seven in Port Hope oldest and of architectural interest, under the auspices of the Architectural Conservancy (Vincent Massey) – a surprising number paid their $2.00 for the privilege of looking. Mona's house has a small oval room on the second floor which she calls her art gallery – we gathered together all the Canadian work we own, including her two and my two "Jacksons".

Yesterday on Bloor street I met Mrs. Guy Mitchell (wife of Roy Mitchell's brother) – she was speaking of you with much admiration.

Best from us
Rody

Toronto – 5,
June 21/1966

NATIONAL ARCHIVES CANADA MG: M630D351; FILE 26; VOLUME 82

Dear Isabel:

Greetings!!!

Do you remember a Mr. Nowry of Ottawa who was here a year (or was it two) ago to make tapings on the Group of Seven for a radio program? He called me to say that this was finally prepared and is to appear under a program called "Venture" on the following dates:

	)July 24/1966 (		
CBC)		(one hour.	Time: 4.03 PM
	)July 31/1966 (		
	)		
	)Also the following Wednesdays.		Time: 11 PM

I understood him to say he had turned in to the Archives, between 30 and 31 hours of materials, worked it down to two hours but that that was too long to fit into a slot of one hour. He said my voice would not be heard on the program as the tapings were too weak and anyway had to be cut because of the above. I do not know if this applies to the taping you made.

He asked me to tell you of this program in case he was unable to contact you.

He asked me to convey his sincere thanks to you.

If you are interested in listening to this I hope the above is the correct information.

With love
Rody

Rosedale Court
Toronto – 5
July 15 – 1966

QUEEN'S UNIVERSITY ARCHIVES: COLL. 2303.37, BOX 6, FILE 19, 1944-1966

Dear Alex:

Greetings!!!

Glad to get your letter of Sept. 15th and to hear you had a good summer – it was one of the best summers we have had for some years, I think. It is quite a feat to work on your holiday and then sell everything before leaving for home – only A.Y.J. could do it.

My attention had been already drawn to your letter in the Ottawa "Journal" about Judy LeMarsh's six million dollar Leonardo – I can hardly imagine Dieffenbaker doing anything but snorting – Mr Pearson more sympathetic but not too concerned.

It will help Blodwen's book a lot with a foreword from you and I think the reproductions you plan would make a valuable record of the "Seven" and a wonderful memorial for Blodwen. I have been looking up my copy (#80) of it, in which Blodwen wrote: "For Rody who also shared the effort and the dream of Tom Thomson, Jan. 24/1936". It is amusingly filled with typographical errors and I wonder for how much of these errors I am responsible as on several occasions, together with Mona Cannon and Franklin Carmichael, I helped to set type for this edition. I know you gave valuable help to Blodwen and it would help if there was an index in the new edition.

…Paul was recalling a time when you were in the country with us and we were battling tent caterpillars by lighting rags on the end of a stick to burn off the nest, with a danger of setting the whole tree on fire. You showed us how you did it: simply poking the stick into the nest and turning the stick, thereby wrapping up the nest with the grubs in it and pulling it down. We were very impressed and used that method from then on.

…We have been tooting around on small trips east and north – Haliburton, Bobcaygeon, Fenelon Falls, etc, and the fall is doing its best to put on a good show – I suppose you are off on another safari of painting.

Best from us, as ever,
Rody

P.S. – I wonder is Blodwen's dedication is to A.Y.J. or F.B.

Rosedale Court –
30 Elm Ave
Toronto – 5
October 20/1966

NATIONAL ARCHIVES CANADA, MG: M630D351; FILE 26; VOLUME 82

Dear Alex:

Greetings!!!

What a beautiful copy of the "Beaver" and what a delightful accompanying article by Naomi, – the color reproductions and the poetry by A.W. Purdy. It will be a most prized number of the "Beaver". Thank you for making us one of the people on your list.

I know I have been owing you a letter for some time but I am sorry to say we have not been having a very good time. We had a happy stay in Delray Beach Florida and arrived home the first week in Feb. and the next week Roy developed phlebitis in his left shoulder, then it went into the right leg and then into the left leg, keeping him slowed up for all of March and April. On May first he had what the doctors call a "mild" stroke, was taken in the ambulance to the emergency, Toronto General Hospital and was in the public ward for almost three weeks. He is home now but the phlebitis came back, from which he is making a steady recovery, but slowly. It has kept us busy and I have not seen many people but I keep in touch with Yvonne, Isabel and Gladys Montgomery by telephone.

I am afraid we will not be going to Expo although we had planned to do so.

…All for now, with best from us both
Rody

Rosedale Court – 204
30 Elm Ave, Tor – 5
Sunday June 25/67

P.S. – As you may remember I have the small picture of yours: "La Maison Abandonnée" and several people over the past year have asked me who has the canvas of this. I think you told me once but I have forgotten
RKC

NATIONAL ARCHIVES CANADA, MG: M630D351; FILE 26; VOLUME 82

Dear Alex:

Greetings!!

I was so glad to see you at "Frances-Florence" studio on Feb. 1 – I was hoping you would be there. It is the only place I have been at night for many months as I do not like driving alone at night, but I was determined to get there. I was disappointed that you did not speak and do some reminiscing about the "Girls", as no one could do it better.

I was very conscious of Frances and Florence all the time I was there, in spite of the changes that have been made. Just between you and me, it was so tidy and only two cats, I am sure Florence and Frances would have been amused. (This is no criticism of those wonderful people who have given it such a lot of care).

With the "girls" gone it leaves a sad gap. Mrs. Radley (who as you remember had a country place close to the "girls" in Scarborough) and I were recalling some of the occasions when they cooked luscious steaks on the outdoor stove and at the same time kept up arguments and conversation with the rest of us. They had their own frank opinions but were never offensive with them. It does not seem possible that they are gone.

I have been reading about Alfred Purdy's book, "Mystery of the Northern Lights", which is to have plates of your canvases but I have not seen the book yet.

It is now over a year since we came home from Florida and Roy immediately developed phlebitis. He seems to have recovered entirely from the mild stroke he had on the first of May, but the phlebitis hangs on and makes walking difficult, but he is steadily improving.

…Signe and Bob McMichael very kindly sent us one of their Christmas greetings, reproducing your "Houses, St. Urbain", a happy surprise.

…I enclose a clipping from last night's Telegram re the discontent that seems to prevail at the Ontario College of Art – there seems to have been a lot of dissatisfaction for some time.

Please, Alex, do not feel that you have to "answer" my letters, but glad to get a note from you anytime.

Very best from us both.
Rody

Rosedale Court – Apt. 204
30 Elm Ave, Toronto – 5,
February 20/1968

NATIONAL ARCHIVES CANADA, MG: M630D351; FILE 26; VOLUME 82

Dear Alex:

Very happy to get a letter from you and to know you are being so well looked after – I hear your apartment is most comfortable and attractive and that you are kept busy giving autographs.

We were very sorry to miss your reception on November 1, and to miss seeing you and Signe and Bob, also Irene Clarke – saw pictures in the press which looked very festive.

I spend practically every afternoon in the hospital with Roy. He is putting up a good fight but I would like to see more improvement.

I do not see very many people as by the time I get home each day I am too tired to be good company for anybody, but they are all very kind and keep in touch by phone.

When things brighten up a little [I] hope to get to Kleinburg among the first things I do.

In the meantime it is wonderful to hear you are so comfortable and enjoying life again after your hospital bout. Best from us

Rody

November 8/1968

NATIONAL ARCHIVES CANADA, MG: M630D351; FILE 26; VOLUME 82

Rosedale Court 204
30 Elm Ave – Tor – 5
Jan 29 – 69

Dear Isabel

Heard you were in the hospital and this is a "well-wish" card to say I hope they are helping to make you comfortable.

Your Christmas card and Co. McLaughlin's arrived and were much appreciated by me – the technique on both cards most interesting.

I had a jaunty Christmas card from Audrey, made by one of her pupils – she has since sent me some of the fibre glass netting with which the card was printed and I hope to have the urge to use it sometime.

…My love to you Isabel
Rody

QUEEN'S UNIVERSITY ARCHIVES: COLL. 2303.37, BOX 6, FILE 17, 1939-1969

Dear Isabel

When I was in Women's College Hosp. over a month ago I received a very beautiful planter – lovely design in the leaves – much admired by other patients and staff, mostly by me.

Hope you are having good health.
With thanks and
L.O.V.E.
Rody

June 14/1973

QUEEN'S UNIVERSITY ARCHIVES: COLL. 2303.37, BOX 6, FILE 20, 1951-1961

LIST
OF WORKS IN
EXHIBITION

St.-Jean-De-Luz Basses – Pyrenees, France c. 1924
oil on board
21.3 x 26.3 cm
COLLECTION OF KAREN MCCARDLE

The Ward 1925
aquatint on paper
12.7 x 11.1 cm (plate); 14.6 x 12.4 cm (sheet)
THE ROBERT MCLAUGHLIN GALLERY; GIFT OF THE
ESTATE OF CHARLES GOLDHAMER, 1985

St. James Chapel, Chicago 1926
sepia etching on paper
16.6 x 20.9 cm (plate); 24.1 x 26.4 cm (sheet)
THE ROBERT MCLAUGHLIN GALLERY; GIFT OF THE
ESTATE OF CHARLES GOLDHAMER, 1985

Untitled 1926
aquatint on paper
10.7 x 13.0 cm (plate); 21.5 x 18.3 cm (sheet)
THE ROBERT MCLAUGHLIN GALLERY; GIFT OF THE
ESTATE OF CHARLES GOLDHAMER, 1985

March Sunlight, Baie St. Paul c. 1929
oil on board
34.7 x 30.1 cm
ONTARIO HERITAGE TRUST, AN AGENCY OF THE
GOVERNMENT OF ONTARIO

Sunday Morning Baie-St.-Paul c. 1929
oil on board
21.6 x 27 cm
RAIN COLLECTION

Sunday Morning – Baie St. Paul c. 1929
oil on canvas
41.1 x 51.3 cm
ONTARIO HERITAGE TRUST, AN AGENCY OF THE
GOVERNMENT OF ONTARIO

Sumach, Lake Superior 1929
linoleum print on paper
14.7 x 15.3 cm (paper); 12 x 14.1 cm (image)
COLLECTION OF KAREN MCCARDLE

Early Morning, Rossport, Lake Superior 1930
mezzotint on paper
11 x 12 cm
RAIN COLLECTION

St. Fidele, P.Q. c. 1930
oil on board
21.5 x 26.6 cm
ONTARIO HERITAGE TRUST, AN AGENCY OF THE
GOVERNMENT OF ONTARIO

St. Fidele, P.Q. c. 1930
oil on canvas
41.1 x 51.2 cm
ONTARIO HERITAGE TRUST, AN AGENCY OF
THE GOVERNMENT OF ONTARIO

Sumachs – Lake Superior c. 1930
oil on pressed board
30.4 x 35.3 cm
ONTARIO HERITAGE TRUST, AN AGENCY OF
THE GOVERNMENT OF ONTARIO

Sumachs – Lake Superior c. 1930
oil on canvas
86.5 x 102 cm
ONTARIO HERITAGE TRUST, AN AGENCY OF
THE GOVERNMENT OF ONTARIO

Cobalt Silver Mine c. 1930-35
oil on board
30.5 x 35.6 cm
PRIVATE COLLECTION

Near Chalk River, Ontario 1933
oil on canvas
86.5 x 101.9 cm
PRIVATE COLLECTION

March Sunlight, Baie St. Paul c. 1935
oil on canvas
61.0 x 71.2 cm
ONTARIO HERITAGE TRUST, AN AGENCY OF
THE GOVERNMENT OF ONTARIO

Tobacco – St. Thomas, Ont. c. 1935
oil on canvas
86.5 x 101.5 cm
PRIVATE COLLECTION

Bog Orchids, Lake Simcoe c. 1936
oil on canvas
61.0 x 45.7 cm
COLLECTION OF CARL AND TRUDY MICHAILOFF

Nella's Horse c. 1936
watercolour on paper
26 x 30 cm
PRIVATE COLLECTION, CALGARY

A.P.K.C. (Paul C.) c. 1937
oil on canvas
53.5 x 46 cm
PAUL COURTICE BESTOWAL COLLECTION TO
THE ROBERT MCLAUGHLIN GALLERY

Grandiflora Blanca c. 1937
oil on canvas
46.0 x 53.7 cm
THE ROBERT MCLAUGHLIN GALLERY;
PURCHASE, 1993

The Silly Ass c. 1937
oil on canvas
77.5 x 62.2 cm
PRIVATE COLLECTION

Fading Trilliums c. 1938
oil on canvas
30.5 x 24 cm
PRIVATE COLLECTION, CALGARY

July Siesta c. 1938
oil on canvas
110 x 122.5 cm
COLLECTION OF TÉRÈSE TÉMOIN DOWNS

Just Cows c. 1939
oil on canvas
91.4 x 99 cm
COLLECTION OF JIL COURTICE

November Pickings c. 1939
oil on canvas
40.5 x 50.7 cm
PRIVATE COLLECTION

Potato Pickers' Rhythm c. 1939
oil on canvas
40.5 x 50.5 cm
PRIVATE COLLECTION

Country Pattern c. 1940
oil on canvas
85 x 70 cm
PRIVATE COLLECTION, CALGARY

The White Calf c. 1941
oil on canvas
72.5 x 87.5 cm
COLLECTION OF KAREN MCCARDLE

Ontario Sugarcane, Markham c. 1942
oil on canvas
50.8 x 50.8 cm
ONTARIO HERITAGE TRUST, AN AGENCY OF
THE GOVERNMENT OF ONTARIO

Boy's Window c. 1942
oil on canvas
60 x 60 cm
CANADIAN FINE ARTS GALLERY, TORONTO

Doves' Dismay 1944
egg tempera on panel
35.4 x 40.6 cm
ART GALLERY OF ONTARIO; PURCHASE, 1944

Country Church – Quebec c. 1945
oil on panel
30.2 x 35.2 cm
COLLECTION OF DIANE WILLEMSE

Parable of the Pigeons 1947
oil on canvas
58.4 x 53.3 cm
HART HOUSE, UNIVERSITY OF TORONTO,
PERMANENT COLLECTION

My Cat c. 1948
oil on canvas
58 x 74 cm
THE ROBERT MCLAUGHLIN GALLERY;
PURCHASE, 2003

The Pet Rooster c. 1948
oil on masonite
40 x 34.5 cm
PRIVATE COLLECTION, CALGARY

The Game c. 1949
oil on canvas
47.2 x 51 cm
THE ROBERT MCLAUGHLIN GALLERY;
GIFT OF ISABEL MCLAUGHLIN, 1989

Dish of Pears c. 1950
oil and egg tempera on panel
25.5 x 30.4 cm
COLLECTION OF KAREN MCCARDLE

Butternut and Pears c. 1950
oil on canvas
27.6 x 37.1 cm
PRIVATE COLLECTION

"Fish Hawkers" Cape Cod c. 1951
oil on board
85 x 100 cm
PRIVATE COLLECTION, CALGARY

Uxbridge Country 1951(?)
oil on canvas
38.2 x 41 cm
THE ROBERT MCLAUGHLIN GALLERY;
GIFT OF J.V. MCKAGUE, 1995

Country Gothic c. 1952
egg tempera(?) on panel
51 x 41 cm
COLLECTION OF DIANE WILLEMSE

Flight c. 1953
oil on masonite
70.9 x 50.6 cm
PAUL COURTICE BESTOWAL COLLECTION TO
THE ROBERT MCLAUGHLIN GALLERY

Sea Horse Ballet c. 1955
watercolour, wax on paper
75 x 60.5 cm
ONTARIO HERITAGE TRUST, AN AGENCY OF
THE GOVERNMENT OF ONTARIO

Canal Composition c. 1962
watercolour on paper laid down on masonite
46 x 53.7 cm
PAUL COURTICE BESTOWAL COLLECTION TO
THE ROBERT MCLAUGHLIN GALLERY

Prairie Wind c. 1963
gold leaf and egg tempera on masonite
102 x 87.1 cm
PAUL COURTICE BESTOWAL COLLECTION TO
THE ROBERT MCLAUGHLIN GALLERY

Crows c. 1960s(?)
watercolour and wax on paper
66.7 x 55.5 cm
ONTARIO HERITAGE TRUST, AN AGENCY OF
THE GOVERNMENT OF ONTARIO

Fairy Larch c. 1966
egg tempera on masonite
92.1 x 61.1 cm
PAUL COURTICE BESTOWAL COLLECTION TO
THE ROBERT MCLAUGHLIN GALLERY

Weather Birds c. 1966
watercolour on paper laid down
on masonite
40.5 x 30.9 cm
PAUL COURTICE BESTOWAL COLLECTION TO
THE ROBERT MCLAUGHLIN GALLERY

Eagle River n.d.
ink on paper
25.1 x 20.1 cm
COLLECTION OF PAUL COURTICE

Farmhouse in Scarborough n.d.
oil on panel
29.3 x 35.6 cm
ART GALLERY OF ONTARIO; GIFT FROM
THE J.S. MCLEAN COLLECTION, BY CANADA
PACKERS INC., 1990

On the River, Bracebridge n.d.
oil on cardboard
29.7 x 34.8 cm
ART GALLERY OF ONTARIO; GIFT FROM
THE J.S. MCLEAN COLLECTION, BY CANADA
PACKERS INC., 1990

Portrait of Mona n.d.
oil on canvas
40.5 x 30.2 cm
PAUL COURTICE BESTOWAL COLLECTION TO
THE ROBERT MCLAUGHLIN GALLERY

Portuguese Fisher Women n.d.
oil on board
31.3 x 38.8 cm
ONTARIO HERITAGE TRUST, AN AGENCY OF
THE GOVERNMENT OF ONTARIO

St. Lit Des Capes n.d.
oil on panel
30.3 x 35.2 cm
COLLECTION OF TOM THOMSON MEMORIAL ART
GALLERY, OWEN SOUND; GIFT OF A.Y. JACKSON

Untitled n.d.
coloured pencils and pastel on paper
11.6 x 15.5 cm
COLLECTION OF PAUL COURTICE

Untitled n.d.
charcoal on paper
25.1 x 20.2 cm
COLLECTION OF PAUL COURTICE

Dorothy Stevens
Canadian, 1888-1966
Conversation Piece of Rody Kenny Courtice c. 1935
oil on canvas
109.2 x 86.5 cm
VARLEY ART GALLERY / TOWN OF MARKHAM

EXHIBITION HISTORY

1925

*The Ontario Society of Artists Fifty-Third Annual
    Exhibition*, Art Gallery of Toronto,
    7-29 March, 1925
    CATALOGUE / BROCHURE PRINTED:
    89. *Monkey Mountain, Port Hope* 90. *In
    the French Pyrenees* (under "Hammond")

The Canadian National Exhibition, Toronto,
    29 August – 12 September, 1925
    CATALOGUE / BROCHURE PRINTED:
    606. *Edward Street* (under "Hammond")

*The Forty-Seventh Exhibition of The
    Royal Canadian Academy of Arts*,
    Art Association of Montreal,
    19 November – 20 December, 1925
    Catalogue / brochure printed:
    99. *Monkey Mountain, Port Hope*
    100. *St. Jean de Luz, France* 291. *Edward
    Street, Toronto* (under "Hammond)

1926

*The Ontario Society of Artists Fifty-Fourth Annual
    Exhibition*, Art Gallery of Toronto,
    6 March – 5 April, 1926
    CATALOGUE / BROCHURE PRINTED:
    150. *Elizabeth Street, Toronto* (under
    "Hammond")

Group exhibition with Edith Coombs,
    Amy Despard, Rody Kenny Hammond
    and Yvonne McKague Housser,
    The Heliconian Club, March, 1926

1927

*The Ontario Society of Artists Fifty-Fifth Annual
    Exhibition*, Art Gallery of Toronto,
    4-27 March, 1927
    CATALOGUE / BROCHURE PRINTED:
    25. *Tobacco Field in Kentucky Hills*

No-Jury Exhibition by Toronto Artists, Simpson
    Galleries, 9-23 April, 1927
    CATALOGUE / BROCHURE PRINTED:
    24. *Mona C.* 25. *Roy C.*

1928

*The Ontario Society of Artists Fifty-Sixth Annual
    Exhibition*, Art Gallery of Toronto,
    3 March – 8 April, 1928
    CATALOGUE / BROCHURE PRINTED:
    24. *Scarecrows*

The Canadian Society of Graphic Art, Art Gallery
    of Toronto, 13 April – 6 May, 1928
    CATALOGUE / BROCHURE PRINTED:
    332. *Snow* 333. *In Kentucky*

The Canadian National Exhibition, Toronto,
24 August – 8 September, 1928
CATALOGUE / BROCHURE PRINTED:
339. Scarecrows

1929

The Ontario Society of Artists Fifty-Seventh
Annual Exhibition, Art Gallery of
Toronto, March, 1929
CATALOGUE / BROCHURE PRINTED:
44. Fire Rangers Hill, Gowganda
45. Old Canal, Cootes Paradise, Hamilton
46. A Sunday Morning, Baie St. Paul

The Annual Exhibition of The Canadian
Society of Graphic Art, Art Gallery
of Toronto, May, 1929
CATALOGUE / BROCHURE PRINTED:
118. An Old House Near St. Patrick's Church

The Canadian National Exhibition, Toronto,
23 August – 7 September, 1929
CATALOGUE / BROCHURE PRINTED:
552. St. Fidele, Quebec 553. Baie St. Paul
554. On the Road to Les Eboullements
895. An Old House Near St. Patrick's

The 51st Exhibition of The Royal Canadian
Academy of Arts, Art Association
of Montreal, 21 November –
22 December, 1929
CATALOGUE / BROCHURE PRINTED:
34. Fire Rangers' Hill, Gowganda 258. Snow
259. Old House Near St. Patrick's Church

1930

The Fifth Annual Exhibition of Canadian Art,
National Gallery of Canada, Ottawa,
23 January – 28 February, 1930
CATALOGUE / BROCHURE PRINTED:
Fire Rangers' Hill, Gowganda

The Ontario Society of Artists Fifty-Eighth
Annual Exhibition, Art Gallery of
Toronto, March, 1930
CATALOGUE / BROCHURE PRINTED:
40. Sumachs, Lake Superior
41. St. Fidele, Quebec

The Canadian Painter-Etchers and Engravers,
Art Gallery of Toronto, April, 1930
CATALOGUE / BROCHURE PRINTED:
Jackfish, Lake Superior, Early Morning,
Rossport, School House, Rossport

The Canadian Society of Graphic Art,
Art Gallery of Toronto, May, 1930
CATALOGUE / BROCHURE PRINTED:
255. At St. Antoine, Quebec

The Canadian National Exhibition, Toronto,
22 August – 6 September, 1930
CATALOGUE / BROCHURE PRINTED:
31. & 370. Sumachs, Lake Superior
371. At Portage, Dufort, Quebec 372. Old
Rectory, Bryson, Quebec 373. Road, Baie St.
Paul, Quebec 567. Jackfish, Lake Superior
568. Early Morning, Rossport, Lake Superior
569. Schoolhouse, Rossport, Lake Superior
570. At St. Antoine, Quebec

1931

The Sixth Annual Exhibition of Canadian Art,
National Gallery of Canada, Ottawa,
15 January – 28 February, 1931
CATALOGUE / BROCHURE PRINTED: Sumachs,
Lake Superior, Jackfish, Lake Superior

The Ontario Society of Artists Fifty-Ninth
Annual Exhibition, Art Gallery of
Toronto, March, 1931
CATALOGUE / BROCHURE PRINTED:
35. Scarecrows, No.2

The Canadian National Exhibition, Toronto,
28 August – 12 September, 1931
CATALOGUE / BROCHURE PRINTED:
386. Scarecrows, No.2 618. The Churchyard,
Springtown, Ont. 619. On the Bracebridge
Road 620. In Bracebridge, Ont. 1
621. On Bracebridge, Ontario 2

Group of Seven Exhibition, Art Gallery of
Toronto, December, 1931
CATALOGUE / BROCHURE PRINTED:
Baie St. Paul, Les Pinettes, St. Fidele

1932

Seventh Annual Exhibition of Canadian Art,
National Gallery of Canada, Ottawa,
22 January – 23 February, 1932
CATALOGUE / BROCHURE PRINTED:
Baie St. Paul

The Ontario Society of Artists Sixtieth
Annual Exhibition, Art Gallery of
Toronto, March, 1932
CATALOGUE / BROCHURE PRINTED: 32. Mona

The Canadian National Exhibition, Toronto,
26 August – 10 September, 1932
CATALOGUE / BROCHURE PRINTED: 196. *On
the River – Bracebridge* 197. *Celery Field in
Scarborough* 198. *A Church in Bracebridge*

1933

The Ontario Society of Artists Sixty-First
Annual Exhibition, Art Gallery of
Toronto, March, 1933
CATALOGUE / BROCHURE PRINTED:
38. *Near Chalk River, Ontario*

The Canadian National Exhibition, Toronto,
25 August – 9 September, 1933
CATALOGUE / BROCHURE PRINTED:
78. *Near Chalk River, Ontario*

The Canadian Group of Painters, Art Gallery
of Toronto, November, 1933; Art
Association of Montreal, January, 1934
CATALOGUE / BROCHURE PRINTED:
91. *La Grotte, Ville Marie, P.Q.*

1934

The Ontario Society of Artists Sixty-Second
Annual Exhibition, Art Gallery
of Toronto, 2 March – 1 April, 1934
CATALOGUE / BROCHURE PRINTED:
27. *Shafts, Northern Ontario* 28. *Log Church,
Deux Rivieres*

The Canadian National Exhibition, Toronto,
24 August – 8 September, 1934
CATALOGUE / BROCHURE PRINTED:
297. *Log Church, Deux Rivieres* 479. *Young-
Davidson Gold Mine, Matachewan*
480. *Frying Pan Lake, Gowganda*
481. *Virgin's Grotto, Ville Marie, P.Q.*

The Fifty-Fifth Exhibition of The Royal Canadian
Academy of Arts, Art Gallery of Toronto,
2 November – 3 December, 1934
CATALOGUE / BROCHURE PRINTED:
49. *Pink House, St. Hilarion, Que.*

1935

The Ontario Society of Artists Sixty-Third Annual
Exhibition, Art Gallery of Toronto,
1 March – 1 April, 1935
CATALOGUE / BROCHURE PRINTED:
35. *Tobacco, St. Thomas, Ontario*

The Artists' Annual Non-Jury Exhibition,
Canadian National Exhibition, Toronto,
Art Gallery of Toronto, 1-15 May, 1935
CATALOGUE / BROCHURE PRINTED:
55. *Railway Town, Lake Superior*
56. *From Up*

The Canadian Society of Graphic Art,
Art Gallery of Toronto, May, 1935
CATALOGUE / BROCHURE PRINTED:
34. *Geese* 35. *Sheep*

The Canadian National Exhibition, Toronto,
23 August – 7 September, 1935
CATALOGUE / BROCHURE PRINTED:
216. *Tobacco – St. Thomas, Ontario*
870. *Shafts* 871. *Teck-Hughes* 872. *O'Brien
Mine – Gowganda* 873. *Old John's House –
Gowganda*

Loan Exhibition of Paintings Celebrating the
Opening of the Margaret Eaton Gallery
and The East Gallery, Art Gallery
of Toronto, November, 1935
CATALOGUE / BROCHURE PRINTED:
92. *Pink Madonna*

1936

Paraskeva Clark, Rody Kenny Courtice, Yvonne
McKague Housser, Isabel McLaughlin and
Kathleen Daly Pepper, The Malloney
Galleries, Toronto, 4-18 January, 1936
CATALOGUE / BROCHURE PRINTED: *March
Sunlight, Tobacco, St. Thomas, Ont.,
On the Gaspe Coast, 100 Year Old House on
Kennedy Road, Near Chalk River, Ont.,
On The River, Bracebridge, Pink House,
St. Hilarion, Que, Sumachs, Lake Superior,
Olive Alina, Donkey and Lilies, La Grotte
and 2 Pussy Willows*

The Canadian Group of Painters, Art Gallery of
Toronto, January, 1936
CATALOGUE / BROCHURE PRINTED:
110. *Geese, St. Urbain*

The Ontario Society of Artists Sixty-Fourth Annual
Exhibition, Art Gallery of Toronto,
March, 1936
CATALOGUE / BROCHURE PRINTED:
54. *Cutting Glory Hole, Young Davidson,
Matachewan* 55. *Bog Orchids, Lake Simcoe*
56. *Ontario No.19*

*The Ninth Annual Exhibition of the Canadian
    Society of Painters in Watercolour,*
    The Canadian Society of Graphic Art,
    The Forty-Fifth Spring Salon of the
    Toronto Camera Club, Art Gallery
    of Toronto, April, 1936; National Gallery
    of Canada, Ottawa, 6 June – 4 July, 1936
    CATALOGUE / BROCHURE PRINTED:
    39. *Nella's Horse* 177. *Shafts in Snow*
    178. *Cobriwi*

The Canadian National Exhibition, Toronto,
    28 August – 12 September, 1936
    CATALOGUE / BROCHURE PRINTED:
    234. *Bog Orchids*

*The Fifty-Seventh Exhibition of The Royal
    Canadian Academy of Arts,* Art Gallery
    of Toronto, November, 1936
    CATALOGUE / BROCHURE PRINTED:
    54. *Lowrey's Cauliflowers, Markham*
    236. *St. Hilarion, Que.*

1937

*The Ontario Society of Artists Sixty-Fifth
    Annual Exhibition,* Art Gallery of
    Toronto, March, 1937
    CATALOGUE / BROCHURE PRINTED:
    37. *Grandiflora Blanca* 38. *Rocks and Trees,
    Whitefish Falls*

*The Tenth Annual Exhibition Canadian Society
    of Painters in Watercolour,* The Canadian
    Society of Graphic Art, The Twenty-
    First Annual Exhibition Society of
    Canadian Painter-Etchers and Engravers,
    The Forty-Sixth Annual Spring Salon of
    the Toronto Camera Club, Art Gallery
    of Toronto, April, 1937
    CATALOGUE / BROCHURE PRINTED:
    29. *Jack McIntosh's House, Markham*
    30. *Repository Plugs, Toronto* 156. *Sheep*
    157. *Milkweed Leaves*

*Exhibition of Paintings, Drawings, and Sculpture
    by Artists of the British Empire Overseas
    (Coronation Exhibition),* Royal
    Institute Galleries, London, England,
    8-29 May, 1937
    CATALOGUE / BROCHURE PRINTED:
    Cauliflowers

The Canadian National Exhibition, Toronto,
    27 August – 11 September, 1937
    Catalogue / brochure printed: 153. *Glory
    Hole, Young-Davidson, Matachewan*

The Canadian Group of Painters, Art Gallery of
    Toronto, 19 November – 19 December,
    1937; Art Association of Montreal,
    January, 1938
    CATALOGUE / BROCHURE PRINTED:
    22. *A.P.K.C.* 22a. *The Silly Ass*

1938

*The Ontario Society of Artists Sixty-Sixth
    Annual Exhibition,* Art Gallery of
    Toronto, March, 1938
    CATALOGUE / BROCHURE PRINTED:
    48. *July Siesta* (noted in brochure as *July*)

*Group exhibition with Dorothy Austin, Rody Kenny
    Courtice, Yvonne McKague Housser, Estelle
    Kerr, Isabel McLaughlin, Kathleen Daly
    Pepper,* The Heliconian Club, March, 1938

*The Eleventh Annual Exhibition of The Canadian
    Society of Painters in Watercolour,
    The Canadian Society of Graphic Art,
    and The Twenty-Second Annual Exhibition
    Society of Canadian Painter-Etchers and
    Engravers,* Art Gallery of Toronto,
    April, 1938; National Gallery of Canada,
    Ottawa, 28 May – 15 August, 1938
    CATALOGUE / BROCHURE PRINTED:
    45. *October, Ontario* 46. *Cherry Pickers,
    Markham* 180. *Paul* 181. *Hillside School,
    Scarborough*

The Canadian National Exhibition, Toronto,
    26 August – 10 September, 1938
    CATALOGUE / BROCHURE PRINTED:
    136. *The Silly Ass* 632. *Paul* 633. *Hillside
    School, Scarborough*

A Century of Canadian Art, Tate Gallery, London,
    England, 14 October – 15 December, 1938
    CATALOGUE / BROCHURE PRINTED:
    Northern Railway Town

*The 59th Exhibition of The Royal Canadian
    Academy of Arts,* Art Gallery of Toronto,
    18 November – 18 December, 1938
    CATALOGUE / BROCHURE PRINTED:
    48. *Vera, Maida and I*

1939

*The Ontario Society of Artists Sixty-Seventh
    Annual Exhibition,* Art Gallery of
    Toronto, 3-29 March, 1939
    CATALOGUE / BROCHURE PRINTED:
    34. *Just Cows* 35. *Stump Fence*

The Fifty-Sixth Spring Exhibition, Art Association
of Montreal, 9 March – 2 April, 1939
CATALOGUE / BROCHURE PRINTED:
84. Grandiflora Blanca 392. Paul

The Canadian Society of Graphic Art,
Art Gallery of Toronto, April, 1939
CATALOGUE / BROCHURE PRINTED:
The Crumply Horn, Lucile, Paul's Frog

The Canadian Society of Painters in Watercolour,
Art Gallery of Toronto, April, 1939
CATALOGUE / BROCHURE PRINTED:
A Cape Cod Church

Canadian Art, The Canadian Society of Painters
in Water-Colour, The Sculptors' Society
of Canada, New York World's Fair,
19 June – 31 July, 1939
CATALOGUE / BROCHURE PRINTED:
32. Cherry Pickers, Markham

Canadian Art, Canadian Group of
Painters, New York World's Fair,
1 August – 15 September, 1939
CATALOGUE / BROCHURE PRINTED:
16. Just Cows

The Canadian National Exhibition, Toronto,
25 August – 9 September, 1939
CATALOGUE / BROCHURE PRINTED:
51. July Siesta (noted in catalogue as July)
380. Paul's Frog 381. The Crumply Horn

The Canadian Society of Graphic Art,
New York World's Fair,
18 September – 31 October, 1939
CATALOGUE / BROCHURE PRINTED:
St. Hilarion, Que.

The Canadian Group of Painters, Art Gallery of
Toronto, October – November, 1939; Art
Association of Montreal, January, 1940
CATALOGUE / BROCHURE PRINTED:
Ontario Pattern, Colts

The Ontario Society of Artists Small Picture
Exhibition, Art Gallery of Toronto,
November – December, 1939
CATALOGUE / BROCHURE PRINTED:
Potato Pickers Rhythm, November Pickings,
The Tractor, Antony

Exhibition of Watercolours by Canadian Artists,
Gloucester, England, 1939

1940

The Ontario Society of Artists Sixty-Eighth Annual
Exhibition, Art Gallery of Toronto,
1 – 31 March, 1940
CATALOGUE / BROCHURE PRINTED:
33. Country Pattern 34. City Pattern

Group exhibition with Rody Kenny Courtice, Bobs
Cogill Haworth, Yvonne McKague Housser
and Isabelle [sic] McLaughlin, The Print
Room, Art Gallery of Toronto,
15 November – 15 December, 1940
CATALOGUE / BROCHURE PRINTED: Just
Cows, Sumachs, The Silly Ass, Geese, Colts,
Flora Blanca, July Cats, Tobacco, Country
Pattern, A.P.K.C.

Small pictures by members of the Ontario
Society of Artists, (in aid of the Canadian
Red Cross) Art Gallery of Toronto,
15 November – 15 December, 1940
CATALOGUE / BROCHURE PRINTED:
Grasshoppers, Cobalt Silver Mine, Ryan
Lake, Matchewan, Rouge River, Cedar Grove

1941

The Sixty-Second Exhibition of The Royal Canadian
Academy of Arts, Art Association of
Montreal, 21 February – 1 March, 1941
CATALOGUE / BROCHURE PRINTED:
18. A Quebec Village

The Ontario Society of Artists Travelling
Exhibition, Elsie Perrin Williams
Memorial Public Library and Art
Museum, February, 1941
CATALOGUE / BROCHURE PRINTED: 38. Haze

The Ontario Society of Artists Sixty-Ninth Annual
Exhibition, Art Gallery of Toronto,
7-31 March, 1941
CATALOGUE / BROCHURE PRINTED:
25. The White Calf

The Canadian Society of Painters in Watercolour,
Art Gallery of Toronto, April, 1941
CATALOGUE / BROCHURE PRINTED: Escape
of a China Horse

The Ontario Society of Artists Small Pictures,
Art Gallery of Toronto, 15 November
– 14 December, 1941
CATALOGUE / BROCHURE PRINTED: Tree
Pattern, Strawberry Planting, Spring Design

The Canadian National Exhibition, Toronto, 1941
CATALOGUE / BROCHURE PRINTED:
The White Calf

1942

The Canadian Group of Painters Exhibition,
    Art Gallery of Toronto, February, 1942
    CATALOGUE / BROCHURE PRINTED:
    17. *Waterfront, November 1941* 18. *Boy's
    Window* 19. *War*

*The Ontario Society of Artists Seventieth Annual
    Exhibition*, Art Gallery of Toronto,
    6 March – 5 April, 1942
    CATALOGUE / BROCHURE PRINTED:
    41. *Ontario Sugarcane, Markham*

*The Canadian Group of Painters Exhibition and
    Sale*, Eaton's-College St. Fine Arts
    Galleries, Toronto, 28 April – 17 May,
    1942 or 1943, no record of works

The Canadian Society of Painters in Watercolour,
    Art Gallery of Toronto, April, 1942;
    National Gallery of Art, Ottawa,
    8 June – 8 July, 1942
    CATALOGUE / BROCHURE PRINTED:
    Ding Dong

1943

The Canadian Society of Painters in Watercolour,
    Art Gallery of Toronto, January, 1943;
    National Gallery of Canada, Ottawa,
    5 March – 4 April, 1943
    CATALOGUE / BROCHURE PRINTED:
    A.P.K.C.'s Mother, R.C.M.P.

*The Ontario Society of Artists Seventy-First Annual
    Exhibition*, Art Gallery of Toronto,
    5-29 March, 1943
    CATALOGUE / BROCHURE PRINTED:
    59. *Wartime Merry-Go-Round*
    60. *Jarvis Street Parade*

1944

*The Ontario Society of Artists Seventy-Second
    Annual Spring Exhibition*, Art Gallery of
    Toronto, 18 March – 9 April, 1944
    CATALOGUE / BROCHURE PRINTED:
    30. *Yvonne McKague Housser* 31. *Autumn
    Orison* 32. *Doves' Dismay*, London Public
    Library and Art Museum, 1944, 13. *Yvonne
    McKague Housser* 14. *Autumn Orison*

The Canadian Group of Painters, Art Gallery
    of Toronto, 21 April – 14 May, 1944;
    Art Association of Montreal,
    7-31 January, 1944; London Art Museum,
    11 February – 7 March, 1944
    CATALOGUE / BROCHURE PRINTED:
    Meatless Tuesday, October Weather

Living Canadian Art, Eaton's-College St. Fine
    Arts Galleries, April, 1944
    ILLUSTRATED IN REVIEW: *Ploughing
    in Quebec*

Pintura Canadense Contemporarnea, Museo
    Nacional de Belas Artes, Rio de Janeiro,
    25 November – 15 December, 1944
    CATALOGUE / BROCHURE PRINTED:
    Boy's Window, Geese, Quebec

1945

*Small Pictures by Members of the Ontario Society of
    Artists*, organized by the Imperial
    Order Daughters of the Empire, Avon
    House Galleries, Simpson's, Toronto,
    26 January, 1945
    NOTED: *Country Church, Quebec*

The Y.M.C.A., War Services Exhibition,
    Canadian Group of Painters, November,
    1945, Sarnia Public Library, after
    November, 1945
    CATALOGUE / BROCHURE PRINTED:
    2. *Spring on Jarvis Street* 3. *Snow Fence*

*The Ontario Society of Artists Seventy-Third
    Annual Spring Exhibition*, Art Gallery of
    Toronto, 3 March – 1 April, 1945
    CATALOGUE / BROCHURE PRINTED:
    29. *Farmer in the Dell* 30. *Toronto
    Electorate 1944-5*

The Canadian Group of Painters Exhibition, Art
    Gallery of Toronto, 23 November
    – 16 December, 1945; Art Association
    of Montreal, 4-19 January, 1946;
    National Gallery of Canada, Ottawa,
    2 March – 30 April, 1946; Winnipeg Art
    Gallery, September, 1946; Saskatoon Art
    Centre, October, 1946; The Edmonton
    Museum of Fine Arts, November, 1946;
    Vancouver Art Gallery, December, 1946;
    Calgary Arts Centre, February, 1947
    CATALOGUE / BROCHURE PRINTED:
    16. *Gentian Alba* (chosen to go on to
    1946-1947 National Gallery of Canada
    Tour) 17. *Rafts on the Rouge River*
    18. *Indian Ancestor*

1946

*The Ontario Society of Artists Seventy-Fourth
Annual Spring Exhibition*, Art Gallery of
Toronto, 9 March – 13 April, 1946
CATALOGUE / BROCHURE PRINTED:
29. *Village in Rouge Valley*

The Canadian Society of Graphic Art,
Art Gallery of Toronto, May, 1946
CATALOGUE / BROCHURE PRINTED:
White Winters

1947

The Canadian Society of Painters in Watercolour,
Art Gallery of Toronto, January, 1947
CATALOGUE / BROCHURE PRINTED:
Autumn Bouquet, Young Hound

Canadian Women Artists, Riverside Museum,
New York, 27 April – 18 May, 1947
CATALOGUE / BROCHURE PRINTED:
14. *The Silly Ass*

The Canadian National Exhibition, Toronto,
22 August – 6 September, 1947
CATALOGUE / BROCHURE PRINTED:
125. *Gentian Alba.*

Solo, Y.W.C.A., Adelaide House, Oshawa,
August, 1947
NOTED IN REVIEWS: *Cows, Pigeons,
Tobacco, Country Pattern, City Pattern,
Wartime Merry-go-Round, La Grotte,
Fanfare, Haze, Coppercliffe, In the
Greenhouse, Farmhouse Near Markham,
Ontario Sugarcane, Grandiflora, October
Weather, Grasshoppers, Bowl With Brush,
Squash, Ontario Village, September
Bouquet, In the Laurentians, Silver Mine*

The Canadian Group of Painters, Art Gallery of
Toronto, 22 November – 21 December,
1947; Art Association of Montreal,
10 January – 1 February, 1948; National
Gallery of Canada, Ottawa, 19 July –
6 August, 1948; Vancouver Art Gallery,
September, 1948; Calgary Arts Centre,
October, 1948; Saskatoon Art Centre,
December, 1948; The Edmonton
Museum of Fine Art, January, 1949
CATALOGUE / BROCHURE PRINTED:
25. *Mines, Northern Ontario*
26. *Irish Ancestor*

1948

The Canadian Society of Painters in Watercolour,
Art Gallery of Toronto, February, 1948
CATALOGUE / BROCHURE PRINTED:
*Blue Madonna, Quebec Church, Farm
Horses and Birch Trees*

*The Ontario Society of Artists Seventy-Sixth
Annual Exhibition*, Art Gallery of
Toronto, 6-28 March, 1948
CATALOGUE / BROCHURE PRINTED:
27. *Country Cat* 28. *Mennonite
Wedding-Day*

4 Women Who Paint, Eaton's-College St. Fine
Arts Galleries, Toronto, 22 March –
3 April, 1948; Adelaide House, Oshawa,
April, 1948
NOTED: *Early Morning, Rossport, (Boy
with) Pet Rooster, Cornflowers, (City)
Pigeons, The Elders Decide* (misattributed
to Haworth in review)

The Canadian National Exhibition, Toronto,
27 August – 11 September, 1948
CATALOGUE / BROCHURE PRINTED:
110. *Indian Ancestor*

*Group exhibition with Paraskeva Clark,
Rody Kenny Courtice, Bobs Cogill Haworth,
Yvonne McKague Housser and Isabel
McLaughlin*, Hart House, Toronto,
October, 1948

Women's Committee Purchase, Sale, Art Gallery of
Toronto, 30 October – 4 November, 1948
*Country Cat, Autumn Ballet, Wild Grapes
and Zinnias*

*Canadian Water Colours Arranged for Showing
in New Zealand*, organized by the
National Gallery of Canada, Ottawa in
co-operation with the Canadian
Society of Painters in Water Colour, 1948
CATALOGUE / BROCHURE PRINTED:
15. *Farm Horses and Birch Trees*

The Western Ontario Travelling Exhibition,
Ontario Society of Artists, 1948-1949
NOTED: *The Pet Rooster*

1949

The Canadian Group of Painters, The Montréal
    Museum of Fine Arts, 8-30 January, 1949;
    National Gallery of Canada, Ottawa,
    8 February – 7 March, 1949; Musée de la
    province de Québec, Québec, 10 March
    – 3 April, 1949; Art Gallery of Hamilton,
    May, 1949; Willistead Library, Windsor,
    13 May – 1 June, 1949
    CATALOGUE / BROCHURE PRINTED:
    14. *Memento Mori*

Canadian Society of Painters in Watercolour,
    Art Gallery of Toronto, January, 1949;
    National Gallery of Canada, Ottawa,
    18 June – 15 August, 1949
    Farm Te Deum

*The Ontario Society of Artists Seventy-Seventh
    Annual Exhibition*, Art Gallery of
    Toronto, 5-27 March, 1949
    CATALOGUE / BROCHURE PRINTED:
    22. *The Game*

*Paintings and Sculpture for the Purchase
    Fund Sale 1949*, Art Gallery of Toronto,
    5-7 November, 1949
    CATALOGUE / BROCHURE PRINTED: *Gentian
    Alba, Autumn Bouquet, Snow Fence*

1950

*The Ontario Society of Artists Small Picture and
    Sculpture Exhibition*, Fine Art Galleries,
    Eaton's College Street, Toronto,
    by January 21, 1950
    CATALOGUE / BROCHURE PRINTED: *Indian
    Remembrance, Dish of Pears, Anglican Rural*

*Exhibition of Contemporary Canadian
    Art*, Art Gallery of Toronto,
    3 March – 16 April, 1950
    CATALOGUE / BROCHURE PRINTED:
    28. *Weathervane* 179. *Two Pears* 320. *Farm
    Weathercock* 321. *Bowl with Fruit*

*The Seventy-First Exhibition of The Royal
    Canadian Academy*, Art Gallery of
    Toronto, 3 March – 16 April, 1950,
    28. *Weather vane*

*Paintings by Doris McCarthy and Rody
    Kenny Courtice*, The London Public
    Library and Art Museum,
    11 October – 14 November, 1950
    NOTED IN REVIEW: *Grandiflora Blanca,
    A.P.K.C., Sunlight, Boy's Window, Just
    Cows, The Elders Decide, Parable of the
    Pigeons, Memento Mori*

The Canadian Group of Painters, Art Gallery
    of Toronto, 10 November – 17 December,
    1950; The Montréal Museum of Fine
    Arts, 3-31 January, 1951; National Gallery
    of Canada, Ottawa; 16 February –
    5 March, 1951
    CATALOGUE / BROCHURE PRINTED:
    29. *Haliburton Accent* 30. *Blessing
    of the Fleet*

Women's Committee Fourth Annual Sale, Art
    Gallery of Toronto, November, 1950
    *Grandmother's Bouquet, Country Parlour,
    River Bank Flowers*

1951

*The Twenty-Fifth Annual Exhibition of The
    Canadian Society of Painters in
    Watercolour*, Art Gallery of Toronto,
    26 January – 4 March, 1951
    CATALOGUE / BROCHURE PRINTED:
    46. *Fisherman's Killicks*
    47. *Country Roadside*

The Canadian Society of Graphic Art, Art Gallery
    of Toronto, March – April, 1951;
    National Gallery of Canada, Ottawa,
    23 May – July, 1951
    CATALOGUE / BROCHURE PRINTED:
    27. *Labrosse Madonna* 28. *Fish*

*Art From Canada, An Exhibition of Canadian
    Painting and Sculpture*, Ontario Society
    of Artists, American British Art
    Gallery, New York, 18 September –
    5 October, 1951
    CATALOGUE / BROCHURE PRINTED:
    9. *City Pigeons*

*The Seventy-Second Exhibition of
    The Royal Canadian Academy of Arts*,
    Art Gallery of Toronto,
    23 November, 1951 – 6 January, 1952
    CATALOGUE / BROCHURE PRINTED:
    22. *Crows on Fall Wheat*

The Canadian National Exhibition, Toronto,
24 August – 8 September, 1951
CATALOGUE / BROCHURE PRINTED:
36. *Mines, Northern Ontario*

Solo, Victoria College, Toronto,
October – November, 1951
NOTED IN REVIEW OR NOTED ON WORK:
*July Siesta, Cows, Grandiflora Blanca,
Fish Hawkers, A.P.K.C., Indian
Remembrance, Boy's Window, Parable
of the Pigeons*

The Canadian Group of Painters, Montréal
Museum of Fine Arts, 1951
CATALOGUE / BROCHURE PRINTED:
26. *Haliburton Accent* 27. *Blessing of
the Fleet*

1952

*The Twenty-Sixth Annual Exhibition of
The Canadian Society of Painters in
Watercolour*, Art Gallery of Toronto,
February, 1952
CATALOGUE / BROCHURE PRINTED:
23. *October Morning, Haliburton*
24. *Tony's Horse*

*The Ontario Society of Artists Eightieth Annual
Spring Exhibition*, Art Gallery of
Toronto, 8 March – 13 April, 1952
CATALOGUE / BROCHURE PRINTED:
21. *Country Gothic*

Exhibition of Graphic Art, Canadian Society of
Graphic Art, Art Gallery of Toronto,
April, 1952
CATALOGUE / BROCHURE PRINTED:
15. *Country Jugs*

The Canadian Abstract Exhibition, Oshawa
Y.W.C.A., 16 October – 10 November,
1952; Hart House, University of
Toronto, 10-24 November, 1952;
Peterborough (location unknown),
December, 1952; Williams' Memorial
Art Museum, London, Ontario, January,
1953; YWCA, Montréal, February, 1953;
Mount Allison School of Fine and
Applied Arts, Sackville, N.B., March
1953; Willistead Library and Art Gallery,
Windsor, May 1 – June, 1953
CATALOGUE / BROCHURE PRINTED:
10. *Blessing of the Fleet* 11. *Georgian
Bay Mood*

*The Sixth Annual Sale of Paintings and Sculpture
by Contemporary Canadian Artists*,
The Women's Committee, Art Gallery
of Toronto, 7-16 November, 1952
CATALOGUE / BROCHURE PRINTED:
Harvesters Resting, Low Tide Loot

*The Seventy-Third Exhibition of The Royal
Canadian Academy*, Montréal
Museum of Fine Arts,
14 November – 7 December, 1952
19. *Country Mousers*

The Canadian Group of Painters, Art Gallery
of Toronto, 31 October, 1952 – 4 January,
1953; Montréal Museum of Fine Arts,
17 January – 8 February, 1953
CATALOGUE / BROCHURE PRINTED:
25. *Fish Hawkers*

1953

*The Twenty-Seventh Annual Exhibition of
The Canadian Society of Painters in
Watercolour*, Art Gallery of Toronto,
9 January – 22 February, 1953
CATALOGUE / BROCHURE PRINTED:
25. *Laurentian Autumn Flowers*

*The Ontario Society of Artists Eighty-First Annual
Exhibition*, Art Gallery of Toronto,
28 February – 30 March, 1953
CATALOGUE / BROCHURE PRINTED:
23. *Flight* (illustrated in catalogue)

*Exhibition of The Canadian Society of
Graphic Art*, April, 1953
CATALOGUE / BROCHURE PRINTED:
21. *Toy Top*

Fourth Annual Sale of Canadian Art,
sponsored by the Women's Committee
of the Windsor Art Association,
Willistead Art Gallery,
20 November – 30 December, 1953
CATALOGUE / BROCHURE PRINTED:
20. *The Game* 21. *Country Gothic*

The Canadian National Exhibition, Toronto,
28 August – 12 September, 1953
CATALOGUE / BROCHURE PRINTED:
24. *Fish Hawkers*

Solo, Heliconian Club, March, 1953

1954

The Twenty-Eighth Annual Exhibition of
  The Canadian Society of Painters in
  Watercolour, Art Gallery of Toronto,
  15 January – 21 February, 1954;
  National Gallery of Canada, Ottawa,
  21 May – 22 June, 1954
  CATALOGUE / BROCHURE PRINTED:
  24. Bowl of Bush Squash 25. Laurentian
  Autumn Bouquet

The Ontario Society of Artists Eighty-Second
  Annual Exhibition, Art Gallery of
  Toronto, 26 February – 28 March, 1954
  CATALOGUE / BROCHURE PRINTED:
  20. Fiddle Heads New Brunswick
  (illustrated in catalogue)

The Annual Exhibition of The Canadian
  Society of Graphic Art, Art Gallery of
  Toronto, May, 1954
  CATALOGUE / BROCHURE PRINTED:
  15. River Net in April 16. Carved Bird and
  Ghost Flowers

The Canadian National Exhibition, Toronto,
  27 August – 11 September, 1954
  CATALOGUE / BROCHURE PRINTED:
  59. Fiddle Heads, New Brunswick

The Canadian Group of Painters Exhibition,
  Art Gallery of Toronto, 19 November,
  1954 – 2 January, 1955; Public Library and
  Art Museum, London, January, 1955;
  Art Gallery of Hamilton, February, 1955;
  National Gallery of Canada, Ottawa,
  16 March – 18 April, 1955
  CATALOGUE / BROCHURE PRINTED:
  17. City Gothic

1955

The Ontario Society of Artists Eighty-Third Annual
  Exhibition, Art Gallery of Toronto,
  7 January – 9 February, 1955
  CATALOGUE / BROCHURE PRINTED:
  17. A Manitoulin Scarecrow (illustrated in
  catalogue) 18. Meadow Seed Pods

The Twenty-Ninth Annual Exhibition of The
  Canadian Society of Painters in Watercolour,
  Art Gallery of Toronto, May, 1955
  CATALOGUE / BROCHURE PRINTED:
  17. Clown 18. Carved Birds and
  Phantom Flowers

The Canadian National Exhibition, Toronto,
  26 August – 10 September, 1955
  CATALOGUE / BROCHURE PRINTED:
  99. City Gothic

The Seventy-Sixth Exhibition of The
  Royal Canadian Academy of Arts,
  Art Gallery of Toronto,
  25 November, 1955 – 2 January, 1956,
  CATALOGUE / BROCHURE PRINTED:
  25. Of the Sea 26. Sea Horse Ballet
  (illustrated in catalogue)

1956

The Ontario Society of Artists Eighty-Fourth
  Annual Exhibition, Art Gallery of
  Toronto, 17 February – 18 March, 1956
  CATALOGUE / BROCHURE PRINTED:
  12. Autumn Flood, Northern River
  (illustrated in catalogue)
  SPECIAL SECTION: Iroquois Interval

The Canadian Society of Painters in Watercolour
  Annual Exhibition, Art Gallery of
  Toronto, 23 March – 22 April, 1956
  CATALOGUE / BROCHURE PRINTED:
  10. Enchanted Cove, Sea Fans and Shells

Exhibition 1956, Canadian Society of
  Graphic Art, Art Gallery of Toronto,
  13 April – 6 May, 1956
  CATALOGUE / BROCHURE PRINTED:
  19. Harborage

The Canadian National Exhibition, Toronto,
  24 August – 8 September, 1956
  CATALOGUE / BROCHURE PRINTED:
  16. Sea Horse Ballet

The Tenth Annual Sale of Paintings and Sculpture
  by Contemporary Canadian Artists,
  The Women's Committee, Art Gallery
  of Toronto, October – November, 1956
  NOTED: Dew on the Grass, Ebbtide
  Loot, Pears

The Seventy-Seventh Exhibition of The
  Royal Canadian Academy, Montréal
  Museum of Fine Arts,
  16 November – 23 December, 1956
  17. In Florida Surf

The Canadian Group of Painters, Art Gallery of
  Toronto, 9 November – 26 December,
  1956 Vancouver Art Gallery, 1957
  CATALOGUE / BROCHURE PRINTED:
  20. Barn Pigeons

1957

The Thirty-First Annual Exhibition of
   The Canadian Society of Painters in
   Watercolour, Art Gallery of Toronto,
   8 February – 3 March, 1957
   CATALOGUE / BROCHURE PRINTED:
   20. *Spring Halloo* (illustrated in
   catalogue)

The Ontario Society of Artists Eighty-Fifth Annual
   Exhibition, Art Gallery of Toronto,
   9 March – 7 April, 1957
   CATALOGUE / BROCHURE PRINTED:
   19. *Celebration* (illustrated in catalogue)

The Seventy-Eighth Exhibition of The Royal
   Canadian Academy of Arts, Associate
   Member, Art Gallery of Toronto,
   15 November – 15 December, 1957
   CATALOGUE / BROCHURE PRINTED:
   20. *Young Spruce Winter*

1958

The Art Gallery of Hamilton Ninth Annual
   Winter Exhibition, Art Gallery of
   Hamilton, February, 1958
   CATALOGUE / BROCHURE PRINTED:
   26. *Larks on Dewy Meadow*

The Ontario Society of Artists Eighty-Sixth
   Annual Exhibition, Art Gallery of
   Toronto, 1-30 March, 1958
   CATALOGUE / BROCHURE PRINTED:
   22. *The Forest* (illustrated in catalogue)

Graphic 58: Twenty-Fifth Anniversary Exhibition of
   The Canadian Society of Graphic Art, Art
   Gallery of Toronto, 2 May – 3 June, 1958
   CATALOGUE / BROCHURE PRINTED:
   110. *In the Garden*

The Canadian Group of Painters Exhibition,
   Vancouver Art Gallery,
   9 September – 5 October, 1958
   CATALOGUE / BROCHURE PRINTED:
   21. *City Gothic*

The Seventy-Ninth Exhibition of The Royal
   Canadian Academy, Montréal
   Museum of Fine Arts, 7 November –
   7 December, 1958, Vancouver Art
   Gallery, 27 January – 22 February, 1959
   24. *Sea Shell Market*

The Ninth Annual Sale of Canadian Art,
   sponsored by the Women's Committee
   of the Windsor Art Association,
   Willistead Art Gallery, 26 November –
   6 December, 1958
   CATALOGUE / BROCHURE PRINTED:
   72. *Mostly Marigolds* 73. *In the Garden*

The Thirty-Third Annual Exhibition of The
   Canadian Society of Painters in
   Watercolour, Art Gallery of Toronto,
   28 November, 1958 – 4 January, 1959
   CATALOGUE / BROCHURE PRINTED: 15. *April*

1959

The Eightieth Exhibition of The Royal Canadian
   Academy of Arts, Musée de la Province,
   Québec, Québec, 6-30 November,
   1959; Civic Auditorium, Winnipeg,
   3-27 January, 1960
   CATALOGUE / BROCHURE PRINTED:
   21. *Northern Channel*

The Canadian Society of Painters in Watercolour,
   Montréal Museum of Fine Arts,
   7-29 November, 1959
   CATALOGUE / BROCHURE PRINTED:
   12. *Spring Halloo*

1960

Art Mart '60, Sarnia Art Association, Guildwood
   Inn, April, 1960
   CATALOGUE / BROCHURE PRINTED: 26. *Ebb
   Tide Loot* 27. *Sailing Vessel, Figurehead*

An Exhibition of Member's Drawing, Canadian
   Society of Graphic Art, Toronto
   Central Library, April, 1960

The Canadian Group of Painters Exhibition,
   Montréal Museum of Fine Arts,
   3 November – 4 December, 1960;
   Norman Mackenzie Art Gallery, Regina,
   5 January – 5 February, 1961
   CATALOGUE / BROCHURE PRINTED: 15.
   Canyon Wall (illustrated in catalogue)

1961

The Ontario Society of Artists Eighty-Ninth Annual
Exhibition, Art Gallery of Toronto,
18 March – 16 April, 1961
CATALOGUE / BROCHURE PRINTED: 16.
Phantom Larch (illustrated in catalogue)

The Canadian Cancer Society Art Exhibition:
Art Through The Ages, CNE Art Gallery,
August – September, 1961
CATALOGUE / BROCHURE PRINTED:
Indian Ancestor

Don Mills Visual Art Association,
North York Public Library,
26 September – 7 October, 1961
Spring Halloo

The Thirty-Sixth Annual Exhibition of
The Canadian Society of Painters in
Watercolour, Art Gallery of Toronto,
24 November, 1961 – 1 January, 1962
CATALOGUE / BROCHURE PRINTED:
22. Larch Seedlings (illustrated in
catalogue)

The Twenty-Eighth Annual Exhibition of
The Canadian Society of Graphic Art,
Art Gallery of Hamilton, 1961
CATALOGUE / BROCHURE PRINTED:
11. Larch in Starlight

Ontario Society of Artists Small Picture Travelling
Exhibition, 1961
NOTED: St. Fidele Road, P.Q.

1962

The Ninetieth Annual Exhibition of The Ontario
Society of Artists, Art Gallery of
Toronto, 31 March – 29 April, 1962
CATALOGUE / BROCHURE PRINTED:
14. Canyon Wall

The Canadian Group of Painters Exhibition, Art
Gallery of Toronto, 10 November –
9 December, 1962; National Gallery of
Canada, Ottawa, 7 March – 7 April, 1963
(or 8 February – 3 March, 1963 according
to Garry Mainprize, "The National
Gallery of Canada: A Hundred Years of
Exhibitions." List and Index, National
Gallery of Canada, new edition
published by RACAR, vol. XI, 1-2, 1984)
CATALOGUE / BROCHURE PRINTED:
8. Canal Carnival

The Thirty-Seventh Annual Exhibition of The
Canadian Society of Painters in Watercolour,
Willistead Art Gallery of Windsor,
23 November – 22 December, 1962
CATALOGUE / BROCHURE PRINTED:
15. Canal Composition

1963

Master Canadian Printers and Sculptors, London
Public Library and Art Museum,
December, 1963; Sarnia Public Library
and Art Gallery, January, 1964
CATALOGUE / BROCHURE PRINTED:
13. Canal Carnival

1964

The Eighty-Fifth Exhibition of The Royal Canadian
Academy, Montréal Museum of Fine Arts,
6-19 November, Sarnia Public Library
and Art Gallery, 8-30 January, 1965
CATALOGUE / BROCHURE PRINTED:
16. Totem Variations

1965

The Canadian Society of Painters in Watercolour
Thirty-Ninth Annual Exhibition, Art
Gallery of Toronto, 8 January –
7 February, 1965; National Gallery of
Canada, 26 February – 21 March, 1965
CATALOGUE / BROCHURE PRINTED:
12. Summer Thunder

The Canadian Group of Painters Exhibition, Art
Gallery of Greater Victoria, 16 March –
4 April, 1965; Agnes Etherington Art
Centre, Kingston, Ontario, 3-27 June, 1965
CATALOGUE / BROCHURE PRINTED:
17. Canal Carnival

1966

Group exhibition with Rody Kenny Courtice, Yvonne
McKague Housser and Isabel McLaughlin,
The Heliconian Club, October, 1966

Small Picture & Sculpture Exhibition, Pollock
Gallery, Toronto, 1966
NOTED: Weather Birds

Women Artists of Toronto, The Canadian
  National Exhibition, Toronto,
  19 August – 9 September, 1966
  CATALOGUE / BROCHURE PRINTED:
  Fairy Larch

1967

The Canadian Group of Painters Exhibition,
  Montréal Museum of Fine Arts,
  19 October – 12 November, 1967;
  Norman Mackenzie Art Gallery, Regina,
  15 February – 10 March, 1968
  CATALOGUE / BROCHURE PRINTED:
  18. *Ocean Reverie*

McLaughlin Public Library, Oshawa, May, 1967
  NOTED: *Fairy Larch, Summer Thunder*

McLaughlin Public Library, Oshawa,
  November, 1967
  NOTED: *Canal Gear*

*The Ontario Society of Artists Members
  Christmas Exhibition and Work's Sale*,
  Albert White Galleries, Toronto,
  16 November – 4 December, 1967
  NOTED: *Of The Sea*

1982

The Canada Packers Collection, Art Gallery of
  Ontario, 27 February – 11 April, 1982
  CATALOGUE PRINTED: *Farmhouse in
  Scarborough, On the River, Bracebride*

1984

The 1940s: A Decade of Painting in Ontario,
  McIntosh Art Gallery, University of
  Western Ontario, London,
  12 September – 7 October, 1984; The
  Gallery / Stratford, Ontario, 12 October –
  11 November, 1984; Laurentian
  University Museum and Arts Centre,
  Sudbury, 20 November – 16 December,
  1984; Art Gallery of Algoma, Sault Ste.
  Marie, 4-27 January, 1985; Timmins
  Museum: National Exhibition Centre,
  Ontario, 8 February – 10 March, 1985;
  Thunder Bay National Exhibition
  Centre, Ontario, 2-28 April, 1985; Art
  Gallery of Ontario, Toronto, 25 May –
  30 June, 1985; Agnes Etherington
  Art Centre, Kingston, 18 August –
  30 September, 1985
  CATALOGUE PRINTED: 18. *Doves' Dismay*

1990

Isabel McLaughlin Gift, Part II, The Robert
  McLaughlin Gallery, Oshawa,
  12 July – 19 August, 1990
  CATALOGUE PRINTED: *The Game, Spring
  Halloo, The White Calf* (all illustrated
  in catalogue)

1993

*Pilgrims in the Wilderness: The Struggle of the
  Canadian Group of Painters (1933-1969)*,
  The Robert McLaughlin Gallery,
  Oshawa, 27 May – 22 August, 1993
  CATALOGUE / BROCHURE PRINTED:
  16. *The Game* (illustrated in catalogue)

1996

Canadian Women Artists, The Arts and Letters
  Club, Toronto, April, 1996
  NOTED: *Country Gothic*

1998

*4 Women Who Painted in the 1930s and 1940s:
  Rody Kenny Courtice, Bobs Cogill Haworth,
  Yvonne McKague Housser and Isabel
  McLaughlin*, Carleton University
  Art Gallery, Ottawa, 9 October, 1998
  – 31 January, 1999
  CATALOGUE PRINTED: 1. *4 Women Who
  Paint* exhibition announcement
  3. *Sumachs* 4. *Untitled* 7. *Cobalt Silver Mine*
  8. *Early Morning, Rossport, Lake Superior*
  18. *Parable of Pigeons* 20. *Grandiflora
  Blanca* 23. *Indian Ancestor* 27. *Laurentian
  Village* 28. *"The things we know, – the
  things we understand"* 33. *The White Calf*
  37. *Sunday Morning, Baie-St.-Paul*
  46. *The Pet Rooster* (numbers 5 and 46
  illustrated in catalogue)

2001

*Modern Woman: Canadian Women Artists Between
  the Wars*, Art Gallery of Hamilton,
  18 January – 1 April, 2001
  Northern Railway Town, Lake Superior

A Community of Artists: Rosa and Spencer Clark
and The Guild of All Arts, Market Gallery,
Toronto, 30 June – 4 November, 2001
Sumachs – Lake Superior, Sumachs – Lake
Superior, St. Fidele, P.Q., St. Fidele, P.Q.,
Portuguese Fisher Women, Sunday Morning
– Baie St. Paul, March Sunlight, Baie St.
Paul, March Sunlight, Baie St. Paul, Ontario
Sugarcane, Markham, Sea Horse Ballet,
Crows, In Canyon Bottom, Canyon Edge

2003

Beyond the Beauty, Nickle Arts Museum,
Calgary, 15 February – 26 April, 2003
Fading Trillium

2005

Lasting Impressions: Celebrated works from the
Art Gallery of Hamilton, Art Gallery of
Hamilton, 25 May – 5 September, 2005;
Art Gallery of Nova Scotia, 5 May –
4 September, 2006; The Beaverbrook
Art Gallery, Fredericton, 23 September –
20 November, 2006; MacKenzie Art
Gallery, Regina, 13 January – 18 March,
2007; Mendel Art Gallery, Saskatoon,
6 April – 3 June, 2007; Museum London,
23 June – 16 September, 2007;
Musée national des beaux-arts du
Québec, Québec, 11 October, 2007 –
6 January, 2008
CATALOGUE PRINTED: *Northern Railway*
Town, Lake Superior (illustrated in
catalogue)

Rody Kenny Courtice:
The Pattern of Her Times

© 2006
The Robert McLaughlin Gallery
72 Queen St., Civic Centre
Oshawa, Ontario L1H 3Z3
www.rmg.on.ca

GRAPHIC DESIGN: Underline Studio, Toronto
PRINTING: Andora Graphics Inc.
PHOTO CREDITS:
Art Gallery of Hamilton: p. 31
Art Gallery of Ontario: p. 79
Collection of Paul Courtice: pp. 12, 15, 21, 23,
40, 42, 46
Michael Cullen, Trent Photographics: pp. all
plates except; JD Photo: pp. 63, 69, 76, 83, 84
Thomas Moore Photography: pp. 20, 22, 31, 45
The Robert McLaughlin Gallery Archives,
gift of Aleen Aked: p. 16
The Robert McLaughlin Gallery Archives,
gift of Isabel McLaughlin: pp. 26, 30, 34, 39, 49, 93

Catalogue of an exhibition held at
The Robert McLaughlin Gallery, Oshawa,
9 November, 2006 – 6 January, 2007;
Varley Art Gallery of Markham, Unionville,
28 January – 18 March, 2007

CURATOR: Linda Jansma

Distributed by: ABC: Art Books Canada,
327 Ste. Catherine W., Suite 229,
Montréal, Québec, H3B 1A2
info@ABCartbookscanada.com

ISBN – 13: 978-0-921500-73-5
ISBN – 10: 0-921500-73-4

1. Courtice, Rody Kenny, 1891-1973.
2. Art Modern–20th century–Exhibitions.
3. Painters–Canada–Exhibitions.
I. Jansma, Linda, 1962- .
II. The Robert McLaughlin Gallery.
III. Title.

759.11

COVER: *The White Calf* (detail)